P9-BYK-175

Contents

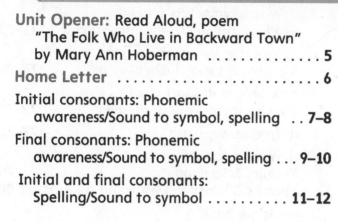

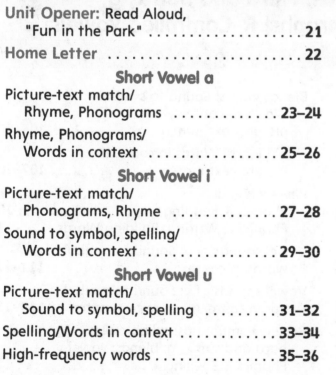

Long Vowels

Theme: On Wings and Wheels

Compounds; le Words; Hard and Soft c, g; Blends; Y as a Vowel; Digraphs; R-Controlled Vowels

Theme: The World Outside

UNIT 5 — Contractions, Endings, Suffixes
Theme: Blasting Off

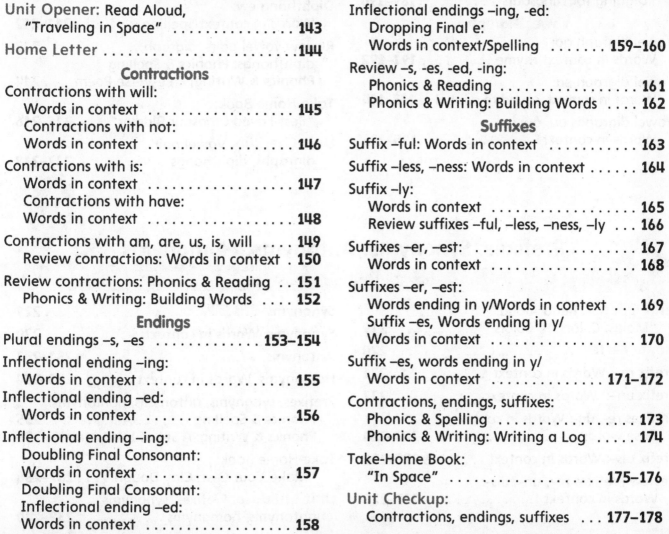

Vowel Pairs, Vowel Digraphs, Diphthongs
Theme: Dinosaur Days

Prefixes, Synonyms, Antonyms, Homonyms
Theme: Make It, Bake It

Read Aloud

The Folk Who Live In Backward Town

by Mary Ann Hoberman

The folk who live in Backward Town
Are inside out and upside down.
They wear their hats inside their heads
And go to sleep beneath their beds.
They only eat the apple peeling
And take their walks across the ceiling.

Why is the town named "Backward Town"?

Dear Family,

In this unit about neighborhood and community, your child will be learning about letters and sounds at the beginning, middle, and end of words. As your child becomes familiar with letters and sounds, you might try these activities together.

▶ With your child, reread the poem "The Folk Who Live in Backward Town" on page 5. Talk about the poem together. Help your child to identify some initial, medial, and final consonant sounds in the poem, such as **p** in peeling, upside, and sleep.

bank
road
car
house

▶ Take a walk through your neighborhood with your child. Point out words on signs and read them aloud. Have your child identify the letters for the beginning and ending sounds.

▶ You and your child might enjoy reading these books together.

The House in the Mail
by Tom and Rosemary Wells

Here We All Are by Tomie de Paola
A 26 Fairmount Avenue Book

Sincerely,

_____

Estimada familia:

En esta unidad, que trata de vecinos y comunidad, su hijo/a aprenderá letras y sonidos al principio, mitad y final de palabras. A medida que su hijo/a se vaya familiarizando con letras y sonidos, pueden hacer las siguientes actividades juntos.

▶ Lean juntos el poema "The Folks Who Live in Backward Town" en la página 5. Conversen sobre el poema y ayuden a su hijo/a a identificar sonidos de consonantes al principio, mitad y final de palabras, como por ejemplo, la **p** en peeling, upside, y sleep.

▶ Caminen con su hijo/a por el barrio y señalen y lean en voz alta palabras en letreros. Pídan a su hijo/a que identifique las letras por los sonidos al principio y al final.

▶ Ustedes y su hijo/a disfrutarán leyendo estos libros juntos.

The House in the Mail
de Tom y Rosemary Wells

Here We All Are de Tomie de Paola

Sinceramente,

_____

Copyright © Savvas Learning Company LLC. All Rights Reserved.

Name _____

 Say the name of each picture. Print the capital and lowercase letters for its beginning sound.

1.
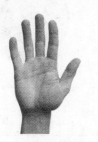

2.

3.

4.

5.

6.

7.

8.

9.

10.

11.

12.

13.

14.

15.

16.

Copyright © Savvas Learning Company LLC. All Rights Reserved.

Say the name of each picture. **Print** the letter for its beginning sound. **Trace** the whole word.

1. ___ ie

2. ___ ig

3. ___ un

4. ___ all

5. ___ in

6. ___ ap

7. ___ ire

8. ___ ive

9. ___ am

10. ___ et

11. ___ ug

12. ___ og

13. ___ ap

14. ___ eb

15. ___ oo

16. ___ ey

Ask your child to name another word with the same beginning sound as each word pictured.

8 Initial consonants: Spelling

Name_____

 Say the name of each picture. Print the letter for its ending sound.

1.

_____

2.

_____

3.

_____

4.

_____

5.

_____

6.

_____

7.

_____

8.

_____

9.

_____

10.

_____

11.

_____

12.

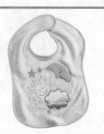

_____

13.

_____

14.

_____

15.

_____

16.

_____

Copyright © Savvas Learning Company LLC. All Rights Reserved.

Say the name of each picture. Print the letter for its ending sound. Trace the whole word.

1. ma

2. we

3. do

4. be

5. sai

6. cu

7. su

8. bu

9. ha

10. lea

11. bo

12. dru

13. li

14. bow

15. bir

16. ja

 HOME Ask your child to find pictures of items whose names have the same ending sounds.

Name _____

> Read **each sentence. Then,** change **the letters to** make new words. Write **the words on the lines.**

cat

1. Change the **c** in **cat** to **m**.

2. Change the **t** to **p**.

3. Change the **m** to **l**.

4. Change the **p** to **d**.

5. Change the **l** to **m**.

6. Change the **d** to **n**.

7. Change the **m** to **r**.

8. Change the **n** to **t**.

Copyright © Savvas Learning Company LLC. All Rights Reserved.

Initial and final consonants   **11**

Say the name of each picture. Print the letter for its beginning sound. Then, print the letter for its ending sound. Trace the middle letter to finish the word.

1. _____ o _____

2. _____ a _____

3. _____ u _____

4. _____ e _____

5. _____ u _____

6. _____ o _____

7. _____ i _____

8. _____ a _____

9. _____ e _____

10. _____ o _____

11. _____ a _____

12. _____ e _____

12 Initial and final consonants: Spelling

 HOME Say each word and have your child think of another word that has the same beginning or ending sound.

Name _____

> Say the name of each picture. Print the letter for its middle sound.

1. 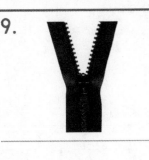	2. 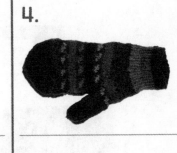	3. 	4. 
5. 	6. 	7. 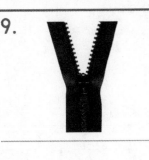	8. 
9.	10. 	11.	12.
13.	14.	15.	16.

Copyright © Savvas Learning Company LLC. All Rights Reserved.

Medial consonants   **13**

Say the name of each picture. Print the letter for its middle sound. Trace the whole word.

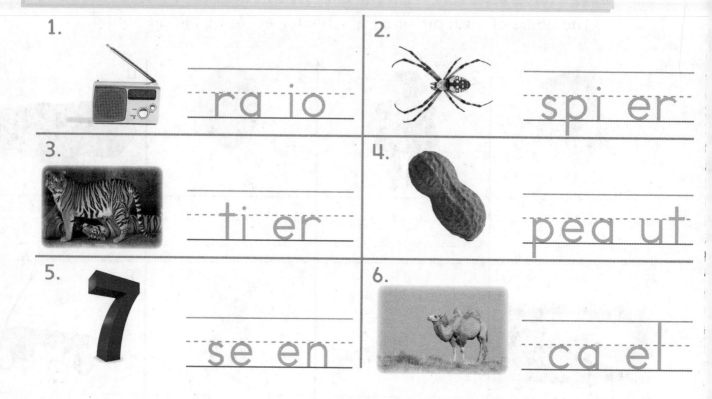

1. ra io

2. spi er

3. ti er

4. pea ut

5. se en

6. ca e

Say the name of each picture. Print the letter for its middle sound. Trace the whole word. Do what the sentences tell you to do.

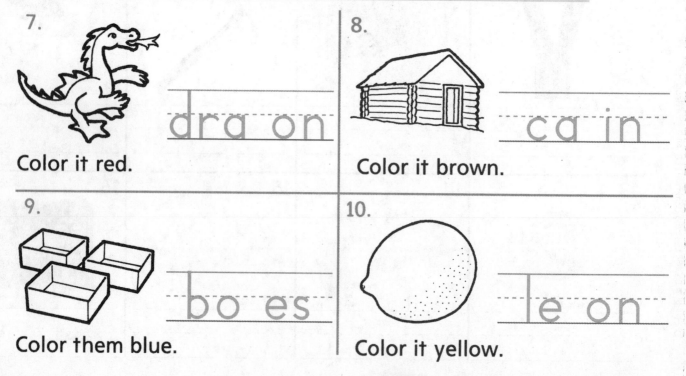

7. dra on

Color it red.

8. ca in

Color it brown.

9. bo es

Color them blue.

10. le on

Color it yellow.

 HOME

Ask your child to find three pairs of words on this page with the same middle sounds.

Name_____

Read **each sentence. To finish the sentence,** use **the mixed-up letters in the box to make a word.** Print **the word on the line.**

1. Pam wants to buy that cute pink _____.

| gpi |

2. Jed wants to get bubble _____.

| ugm |

3. I wonder what is in that big _____.

| oxb |

4. Mom wants a yellow _____.

| elmno |

5. Did Dad find a jar of _____ yet?

| maj |

6. I will buy this blue _____.

| pne |

7. Can that _____ fly high?

| ekit |

8. Look, there is a spider _____!

| bwe |

9. Is there a _____ in it?

| edrips |

10. I _____ that is not for sale!

| ebt |

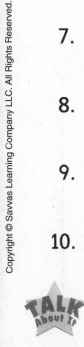

What are Jed and his family doing?

Initial, medial, final consonants: Spelling, high-frequency words, critical thinking   **15**

Copyright © Savvas Learning Company LLC. All Rights Reserved.

When you **describe an event**, you name the thing that happened and tell where it took place. Then, you write about the things that happened in the order they took place.

Think about something that happened in your neighborhood, school, or community, such as a parade or a fair. Use sentences to tell about it. Then, tell how you felt about the things that happened. The words in the box may help you.

bird	man	spider	car	kitten
duck	bus	ball	log	box
dog	book	web	bug	zoo

Name the event you are telling about.

Tell where things took place.

Name things that happened in the order they took place.

Name _____

Copyright © Savvas Learning Company LLC. All Rights Reserved.

Home Sweet Home!

Everyone needs a place to live!
In many large cities, people live in
tall apartment buildings.

1

- - - FOLD -

Maybe houses of the future will
be bubbles, towers, or rockets in
space. Computers will probably be
used to help with household tasks.
The sun's energy may be used for
heat and light. What do you think?

4

Some people take their homes from place to place. In Asia, many herders travel with their goats and sheep to find food for them. The herders carry their homes, called *yurts*, with them.

2

--- FOLD ---

A houseboat is a home that stays in the water all year long. Some people in the United States, Europe, and many parts of Asia live on houseboats. In China these boats are known as *sampans*.

3

Name _____

Copyright © Savvas Learning Company LLC. All Rights Reserved.

 Say the name of each picture. Fill in the bubble beside the letter for the **beginning sound** of the word.

1.
○ b
○ g
○ d

2.
○ k
○ m
○ y

3.
○ w
○ r
○ t

4.
○ w
○ l
○ m

 Say the name of each picture. Fill in the bubble beside the letter for the **ending sound**.

5.
○ b
○ l
○ s

6.
○ d
○ x
○ g

7.
○ m
○ b
○ x

8.
○ m
○ p
○ b

 Say the name of each picture. Fill in the bubble beside the letter for the **middle sound**.

9.
○ r
○ c
○ b

10.
○ c
○ t
○ r

11.
○ m
○ n
○ l

12.
○ r
○ d
○ l

Initial, medial, final consonants: Assessment   **19**

Circle the word that answers the riddle.
Print it on the line.

1. I rhyme with **ham.** I am _____.

jam
car
farm

2. I rhyme with **drum.** I am _____.

gas
gull
gum

3. A spider spins me. I am a _____.

web
well
wet

4. I say "oink." I am a _____.

big
pig
fig

5. I come after six. I am _____.

seven
tiger
robot

6. I rhyme with **fox.** I am a _____.

bag
box
bell

7. You can write with me. I am a _____.

pet
peg
pen

8. You can ride in me. I am a _____.

cabin
wagon
lemon

 With your child, take turns making up riddles using the words on this page.

Read Aloud

Fun in the Park

New York is a big city. People work hard. They also have fun. Many people go to Central Park to have fun. The park is in the middle of the city.

Kids play baseball in the park. Some people sail boats, ride bikes, or jog. Families go to the park to have a picnic or visit the zoo.

In the winter, many families skate on one of two ice-skating rinks. Others go sledding or play in the snow.

TALK About It

What would you like to do in Central Park? Why?

Dear Family,

In this unit "At Work, At Play," your child will be learning to read and write words with short vowel sounds. The names of many things we do for work and fun contain short vowel sounds such as sit, hop, run, bend, clap. As your child explores the short vowel sounds, you might like to try these activities together.

Estimada familia:

En esta unidad, titulada "Trabajando, jugando" ("At Work, At Play"), su hijo/a aprenderá a leer y escribir palabras con sonidos breves. Los nombres de muchas actividades que realizamos cuando trabajamos o jugamos contienen vocales con sonidos breves, como por ejemplo, sit (sentarse), hop (saltar), run (correr), bend (inclinarse), clap (aplaudir). A medida que su hijo/a se vaya familiarizando con las vocales de sonido breve, pueden hacer las siguientes actividades juntos.

a clap

e bend

i skip

o hop

u run

▶ Reread the selection on page 21 with your child. Talk about life in a city. Help your child to find the words that contain a short vowel sound.

▶ Play a riddle game with your child. Think up a riddle whose answer is a short vowel word; for example: I am what you do with a song. What am I? (sing)

You and your child might enjoy reading these books together.

Busy, Busy City Street
by Cari Meister

The Great Ball Game
by Joseph Bruchac

Sincerely,

▶ Lean con su hijo/a la selección en la página 21. Hablen sobre la vida en una ciudad. Ayuden a su hijo/a a hallar las palabras que contienen una vocal con sonido breve.

▶ Jueguen con su hijo/a a las adivinanzas. Inventen una adivinanza cuya respuesta tenga una palabra con sonido breve; como por ejemplo, I am what you do with a song. What am I? (sing)

Ustedes y su hijo/a disfrutarán leyendo estos libros juntos.

Busy, Busy City Street
de Cari Meister

The Great Ball Game
de Joseph Bruchac

Sinceramente,

Copyright © Savvas Learning Company LLC. All Rights Reserved.

Name _____

Fast, fast, fast.
My taxi goes so fast!
I can slow my cab down
As I get close to town.

RULE

If a word or syllable has only one vowel, and it comes at the beginning of a word or between two consonants, the vowel is usually short. You can hear the short **a** sound in **fast**.

▶ Circle **the name of each picture.**

1.
hat   ham

hand   had

2.
bag   hat

bat   bad

3.
camp   lad

lap   lamp

4.
sad   back

bag   bat

5.
cat   cap

cab   can

6.
and   an

at   ant

7.
mat   man

pan   map

8.
cat   can

cab   cap

9.
mad   ram

rack   mat

Copyright © Savvas Learning Company LLC. All Rights Reserved.

Short vowel a   **23**

Draw a line through three words that rhyme in each box. Lines can go across, up and down, or on a diagonal.

1.

ram	cab	gas
sad	ham	tag
bad	fan	yam

2.

ax	lap	hat
wax	map	can
bag	nap	had

3.

dad	tap	pal
bat	sat	cat
mat	pan	cap

4.

tax	fat	tag
mad	wag	tab
bag	pad	sag

24   Short vowel a: Phonograms

HOME Help your child think of another word to add to each group of rhyming words.

Name _____

▶ Find **words** in the box that **rhyme** with each child's name.
Print the rhyming words above or below each child's picture.

cat	ham	dad	fan	jam	van	hat	bad
sad	pan	yam	mat	can	bat	had	ram

1.

2.

3.

4.

Short vowel a: Phonograms   **25**

Copyright © Savvas Learning Company LLC. All Rights Reserved.

Circle **the word that will finish each sentence.** Print **it on the line.**

1. I am Sam, and my cat is _____.   camp   Pat   cart

2. Pat likes milk and _____ food.   class   sat   cat

3. She eats a lot, but she is not _____.   van   fat   lamp

4. She likes to lick my _____.   hand   gas   band

5. Pat likes to sit on my _____.   lap   ham   Sam

6. Pat does not like to have a _____.   gap   bath   rack

7. She runs away as _____ as she can.   fast   class   bat

8. I _____ always find her.   can   past   fast

9. She takes a nap on a _____.   mast   mat   fat

10. She takes a _____ on Dad's lap.   ran   sat   nap

11. I _____ happy that Pat is my cat.   can   am   as

 Do you think Pat likes Sam? Why or why not?

 Help your child think of words that rhyme with the answers he or she used in the sentences.

Name _____

We will visit the city.
We will sit in the stands.
We will see the ball hit.
We will cheer with the fans.

RULE

If a word or syllable has only one vowel, and it comes at the beginning of a word or between two consonants, the vowel is usually short. You can hear the short **i** sound in **sit** and **in**.

▶ **Circle the name of each picture.**

1.

sack
milk
mill
tap

2.

mitt
fat
mat
mill

3.

wind
tag
wig
wag

4.

lap
lips
nap
dill

5.

bag
pig
fig
pat

6.

hill
bill
sill
hat

7.

tax
six
fix
sat

8.

bill
bit
hat
bib

9.

wink
sank
sink
pink

Copyright © Savvas Learning Company LLC. All Rights Reserved.

Short vowel i   **27**

► **Color** the parts of each ball with rhyming words the same color.

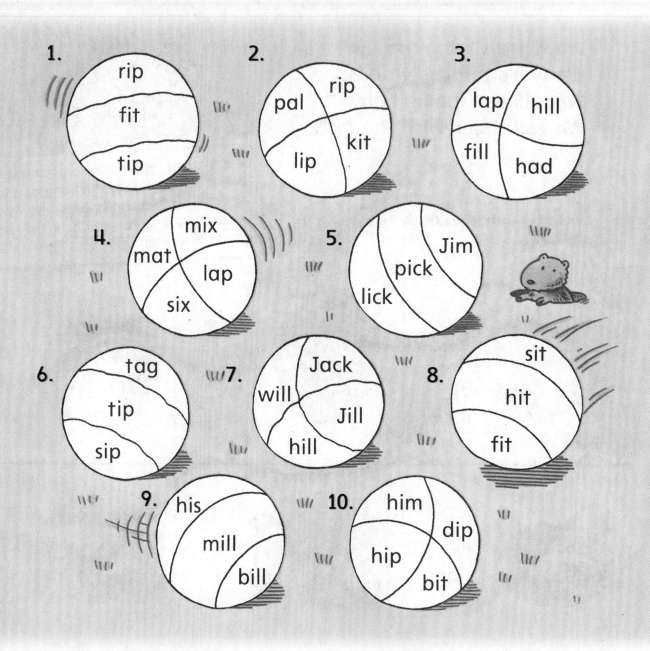

1. rip fit tip

2. pal rip lip kit

3. lap hill fill had

4. mix mat lap six

5. Jim pick lick

6. tag tip sip

7. Jack will Jill hill

8. sit hit fit

9. his mill bill

10. him dip hip bit

► **Use some of the rhyming words to write a sentence.**

_____

- - - - - - - - - - - - - - - - - - -

_____

- - - - - - - - - - - - - - - - - - -

_____

HOME With your child, take turns making up sentences using the rhyming words on each ball.

Name _____

> Print the word in the box that names each picture.
> In the last box, draw a picture of a short vowel
> word. Print the picture name.

1.

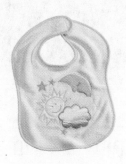

_____
- - - - - - - - - - -
_____

2.

_____
- - - - - - - - - - -
_____

3.

_____
- - - - - - - - - - -
_____

4.

_____
- - - - - - - - - - -
_____

5.

_____
- - - - - - - - - - -
_____

6.

_____
- - - - - - - - - - -
_____

7.

_____
- - - - - - - - - - -
_____

8.

_____
- - - - - - - - - - -
_____

9.

_____
- - - - - - - - - - -
_____

10.

_____
- - - - - - - - - - -
_____

11.

_____
- - - - - - - - - - -
_____

12.

_____
- - - - - - - - - - -
_____

Copyright © Savvas Learning Company LLC. All Rights Reserved.

Short vowel i: Spelling   **29**

Circle **the word that answers each riddle.** Print **it on the line.**

1. It can swim.
   What is it?

---

fast   fish

fix   fat

2. We drink it.
   What is it?

---

mitt   man

milk   mat

3. It comes after five.
   What is it?

---

sink   sad

sat   six

4. It rhymes with **bill.**
   What is it?

---

hit   hat

hill   ham

5. Lunch goes on it.
   What is it?

---

dad   dish

dig   did

6. It has a funny tail.
   What is it?

---

pin   pig

pal   pat

7. It fits on a finger.
   What is it?

---

rank   rat

rip   ring

8. A baby wears this.
   What is it?

---

bib   bad

bill   bat

9. I play ball with it.
   What is it?

---

mat   mitt

map   mix

 Ask your child to name a word that rhymes with the answer to each riddle.

Name _____

I will jump, you will run.
We will play in the morning sun.
What great fun, thanks a bunch!
Now it is time to have some lunch!

> **Circle the name of each picture.**
> **Print the vowel you hear in the word you circled.**

RULE

If a word or syllable has only one vowel, and it comes at the beginning of a word or between two consonants, the vowel is usually short. You can hear the short **u** sound in **run** and **lunch**.

1. cap · cup _____ kit _____	**2.** gas · gull _____ gum _____	**3.** Dick · duck _____ dad _____
4. can · cup _____ cap _____	**5.** as · bun _____ bus _____	**6.** bag · tip _____ bug _____
7. not · nut _____ nap _____	**8.** sun · sum _____ dim _____	**9.** tab · but _____ bat _____

Copyright © Savvas Learning Company LLC. All Rights Reserved.

Short vowel u   **31**

Say the name of each picture. Print the name on the line.

1.

2.

3.

4.

5.

6.

7.

8.

9.

10.

11.

12.

Short vowel u: Spelling

 HOME

Have your child make up silly sentences with rhyming words from the page. Include other rhyming words.

Name _____

▶ Read the words in the box. Print a word in the puzzle to name each picture.

run	tub	bun	bug
rug	cub	sun	nut

Across ➡

2.

4.

6.

7.

Down ⬇

1.

3.

5.

6.

▶ Write a silly sentence about something that could happen on a hot summer day. Use short **u** words from the puzzle.

_____

- -

_____

- -

_____

Copyright © Savvas Learning Company LLC. All Rights Reserved.

Circle **the word that will finish the sentence.**
Print **it on the line.**

1. Today there was a fuss on the ＿＿＿＿＿＿＿.

run
bus
must

2. A ＿＿＿＿＿＿ jumped on Gus.

us
bug
hug

3. Gus jumped ＿＿＿＿＿＿.

run
cup
up

4. Then, it jumped on ＿＿＿＿＿＿.

bus
hug
Russ

5. I saw the bug ＿＿＿＿＿＿ on the window.

just
jump
rust

6. It was ＿＿＿＿＿＿ a little bug.

just
cup
up

7. It liked to ＿＿＿＿＿＿ up and down the window.

rug
run
cup

8. The bug ＿＿＿＿＿＿ like to ride on the bus.

run
us
must

 **What would you do if
you were on the bus?**

 Ask your child to say and spell the
words he or she did not write in
the sentences.

Short vowel u: High-frequency words, critical thinking

Name _____

does	about
our	other
Then	Where

1. What _____ an ant eat?

2. _____ can we find the facts?

3. We can look in this book _____ ants.

4. It tells about _____ bugs, too.

5. _____, we can go out and see some ants.

6. We can take _____ book with us.

Copyright © Savvas Learning Company LLC. All Rights Reserved.

Look at the words in the box. Find each word in the puzzle, and circle it. The words go across and down. Then, write the words on the lines.

does	about
our	other
then	where

o	a	b	o	u	t
u	n	v	t	o	h
r	e	p	h	d	e
y	d	o	e	s	n
w	h	e	r	e	r

1. _____

2. _____

3. _____

4. _____

5. _____

6. _____

CHECKING UP

Put a ✔ next to each word you can read.

☐ does ☐ about ☐ our ☐ other ☐ then ☐ where

HOME Help your child use each word in a sentence that asks a question.

Name _____

 **Phonics & Reading**

Copyright © Savvas Learning Company LLC. All Rights Reserved.

Read the story. Print a short a, i, or u word from the story to finish each sentence.

Playing Soccer

Do you like to run, kick a ball, and have lots of fun? Then, soccer is just the game for you!

A soccer field has a net at each end. Two teams of players run and pass the ball to other players on their team. Then, they try to hit or kick the ball into a net. They can use their feet, chests, and heads but not their hands.

A player called the goalie tries to stop the ball. It can be a hard job! Does this game sound like a winner? Kids across the land think so. So do the fans in the stands!

1. Soccer players _____ on a field and _____ a ball.

2. They can use their feet, but they cannot use their _____.

3. The game is a big hit with kids and their _____.

 TALK About It What does a team need to do to win the game?

Use **a letter tile to make a word with at, ip, ing or ut.** Write **each real word on the lines.**

c s z m r

at

1. cat

2. _____

3. _____

4. _____

c s r z n

ip

5. _____

6. _____

7. _____

8. _____

w s r n k

ing

9. _____

10. _____

11. _____

12. _____

r n c v b

ut

13. _____

14. _____

15. _____

16. _____

 Ask your child to choose two words from each group and use them in a silly sentence.

Name _____

Put it in the pot,
Shake it 'til it's hot.
Pop! Pop! Pop!
See the popcorn hop!

▶ Say **the name of each picture.** Print **the name on the line.**

RULE

If a word or syllable has only one vowel, and it comes at the beginning of a word or between two consonants, the vowel is usually short. You can hear the short **o** sound in **pop** and **hot**.

1.

_ _ _ _ _ _ _ _ _ _ _ _

2.

_ _ _ _ _ _ _ _ _ _ _ _

3.

_ _ _ _ _ _ _ _ _ _ _ _

4.

_ _ _ _ _ _ _ _ _ _ _ _

5.

_ _ _ _ _ _ _ _ _ _ _ _

6.

_ _ _ _ _ _ _ _ _ _ _ _

7.

_ _ _ _ _ _ _ _ _ _ _ _

8.

_ _ _ _ _ _ _ _ _ _ _ _

9.

_ _ _ _ _ _ _ _ _ _ _ _

10.

_ _ _ _ _ _ _ _ _ _ _ _

11.

_ _ _ _ _ _ _ _ _ _ _ _

12.

_ _ _ _ _ _ _ _ _ _ _ _

Copyright © Savvas Learning Company LLC. All Rights Reserved.

► **Circle the name of each picture.**

1.

fix
cob
fox
six

2.

pot
top
tap
pit

3.

bill
sill
dill
doll

4.

fox
fix
box
bat

5.

dog
dug
dig
pot

6.

rock
sit
sack
sock

7.

pig
pop
pup
pat

8.

lag
log
bug
lot

9.

luck
lock
lick
lack

10.

mop
map
mud
milk

11.

ham
hit
hot
hut

12.

fix
tax
ax
ox

40   **Short vowel o**

 HOME

Have your child find the pictures on this page and on page 39 whose names rhyme.

Name _____

► Help **the frog hop to the pond.** Look **at each picture.**
Write **the name of each picture on the line.**

| top | dog | box | sock | |
| lock | rock | log | fox | pot |

Copyright © Savvas Learning Company LLC. All Rights Reserved.

Short vowel o   **41**

Fill in the bubble beside the sentence that tells about the picture. Then draw a circle around each short o word in the sentences.

1.
- ○ The fox is not in the log.
- ○ The fox is in the log.
- ○ The fox is on the log.
- ○ The fox is under the log.

2.
- ○ Rob lost his sock.
- ○ Rob sat on a big rock.
- ○ Rob is on the big log.
- ○ Rob has a big rock in his hand.

3.
- ○ The dog ran over the box.
- ○ The mop is not in the box.
- ○ I will hop on the log.
- ○ See the doll in the box.

4.
- ○ I got the mop for Don.
- ○ Jill has the small top.
- ○ The small top is on the mop.
- ○ The top is in Bob's hand.

5.
- ○ The hot pot is on the table.
- ○ Dot is not holding a hot pot.
- ○ Dot is holding a hot pot.
- ○ The pot Dad is holding is not hot.

HOME Ask your child to read a sentence that is not pictured and draw a picture for it.

Name_____

I like to spend a sunny day
Getting shells at the bay,
Or playing with my friend,
Hoping today will not end!

> Say **the name of each picture. Print the name on the line.**

RULE

If a word or syllable has only one vowel, and it comes at the beginning of a word or between two consonants, the vowel is usually short. You can hear the short **e** sound in **spend** and **shells.**

1.
_____

2.
_____

3.
_____

4.
_____

5.
_____

6.
_____

7.
_____

8.
_____

9.
_____

10.
_____

11.
_____

12.
_____

Copyright © Savvas Learning Company LLC. All Rights Reserved.

▶ **Print the name of each picture. Then, do what the sentences tell you to do.**

1.

2.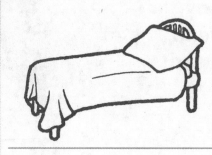

3.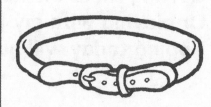

4.

5.

6.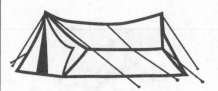

Find the bed.
Color it red
and blue.

Find the jet.
Color it black.

Find the nest.
Color the
eggs blue.

Find the tent.
Color it yellow.

Find the belt.
Color it green.

Find the vest.
Color it red
and black.

44   Short vowel e

 HOME

Ask your child to find the names
of two colors on this page that
have the short e sound.

Name _____

▶ Fill in **the bubble below the word that will finish each sentence. Print the word on the line.**

1. My name is _____.

   men   Jeff   jet
   ○   ○   ○

2. I want to get a _____.

   bet   pet   yet
   ○   ○   ○

3. I would like a pet dog _____.

   rest   west   best
   ○   ○   ○

4. I will _____ take care of my pet.

   help   bell   nest
   ○   ○   ○

5. I can take it to the _____.

   vet   bet   set
   ○   ○   ○

6. I will make sure it is _____.

   get   fed   bed
   ○   ○   ○

7. It will need a good _____.

   bed   nest   best
   ○   ○   ○

8. I will _____ it in and out.

   jet   test   let
   ○   ○   ○

9. I can dry it when it's _____.

   net   wet   set
   ○   ○   ○

10. I will _____ it if I get it.

    sled   pet   west
    ○   ○   ○

11. I might name my pet _____.

    Pepper   fed   set
    ○   ○   ○

12. I will _____ Ned about my pet.

    sell   tell   fell
    ○   ○   ○

TALK About It Why would Jeff make a good pet owner?

Short vowel e: High-frequency words, critical thinking   **45**

Copyright © Savvas Learning Company LLC. All Rights Reserved.

► **Print** the name of each picture on the line.

1.	2.	3.	4.	5.

► **Print yes or no on the line to answer each statement.**

6. You can sit in a tent. _____

7. A hen can lay eggs. _____

8. A cat has six legs. _____

9. A big bus can jump up and down. _____

10. You can go fast in a jet. _____

11. An ant is as big as an ox. _____

12. Six is less than ten. _____

13. You can rest in a bed. _____

14. You have ten fingers and ten toes. _____

46   Short vowel e: Spelling

Ask your child to circle and read
the short e words in each sentence.

Name_____

▶ **Read** the words in the box. **Write** a word to finish each sentence.

Would	care
because	under
sure	good

1. Hide-and-seek is a _____ game to play.

2. I am _____ that I will find you.

3. I will find you _____ I will look everywhere!

4. I see Jan hiding _____ the bush.

5. Sam does not _____ that I see him by the shed.

6. _____ you like to play again? Now find me!

Copyright © Savvas Learning Company LLC. All Rights Reserved.

▶ **Print** a word in the puzzle for each clue.
Use the words in the box.

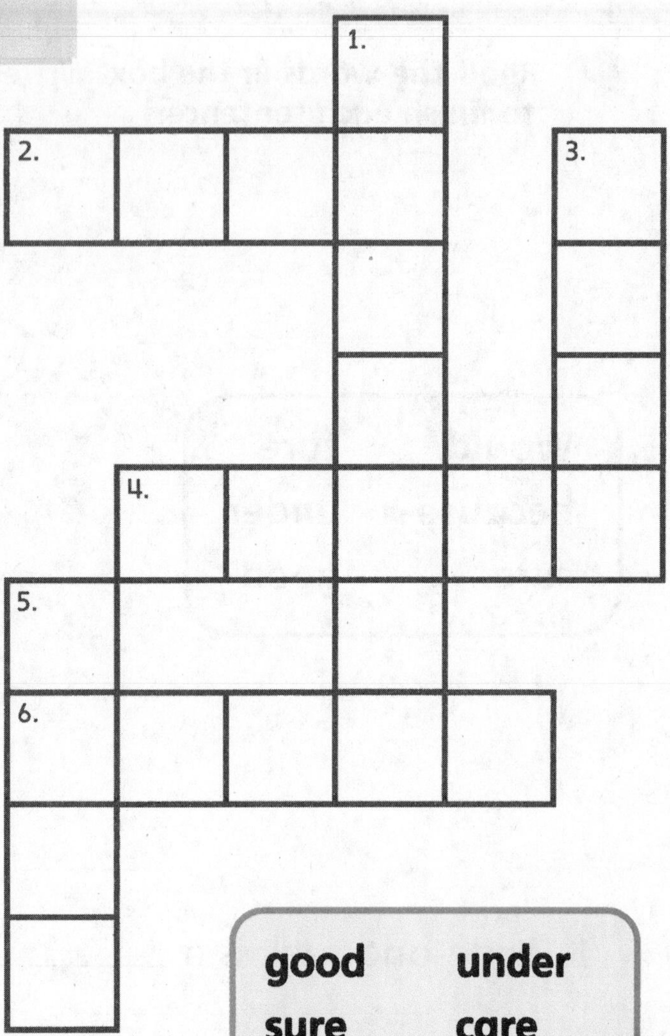

ACROSS

2. We should take——— of our pets.

4. This word rhymes with **could**.

6. If it's not over, it's ————.

DOWN

1. This word tells why.

3. If it's not bad, it's ————.

5. If you have made up your mind, you are————.

good	under
sure	care
because	would

CHECKING UP

▶ Put a ✔ next to each word you can read.

☐ would ☐ care ☐ because ☐ under ☐ sure ☐ good

HOME
Ask your child to read the clues and the answers aloud.

Name _____

Phonics & Spelling

Say and spell each short vowel word. Print the word on the banner of the plane that shows its short vowel sound.

net	wig	ox	cab	bun
ram	nut	doll	leg	dish
lips	web	ax	sun	box

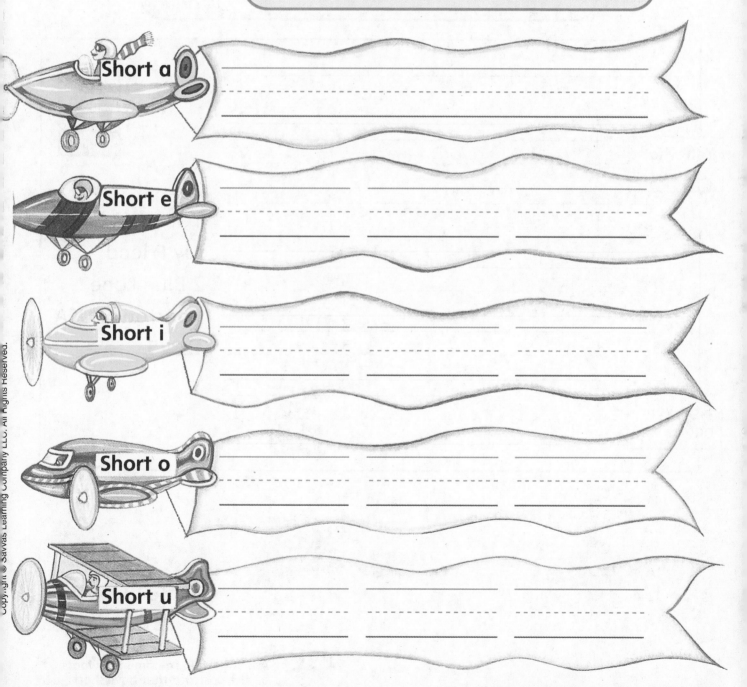

Short a

Short e

Short i

Short o

Short u

Short vowels a, i, u, o, e   **49**

Copyright © Savvas Learning Company LLC. All Rights Reserved.

A **postcard** is a way of sending a short message to a friend while you are away on vacation. It uses words that tell the friend that you are having fun.

▶ Use **some of the words in the box to** write **a postcard telling a friend about the fun you had at the beach.**

dig	fun	swim	hot	camp
run	net	doll	sand	pet

Tell what you did.

TO:

My Friend

2 Blue Lane

Yourtown, USA

12345

Sign your name.

Ask your child to name the words on the postcard that have short vowel sounds.

Copyright © Savvas Learning Company LLC. All Rights Reserved.

Name _____

Hello From Camp!

July 10

Dear Mom and Dad,

Well, here I am at Camp Windsong! The bus ride was fun. We talked and laughed, and I made a new friend, Beth.

1

FOLD

After dinner, we sat around the campfire, played games, and sang songs. I am having a great time. Please write soon.

Love,

Jill

4

Review short vowels a, i, u, o, e: Take-home book

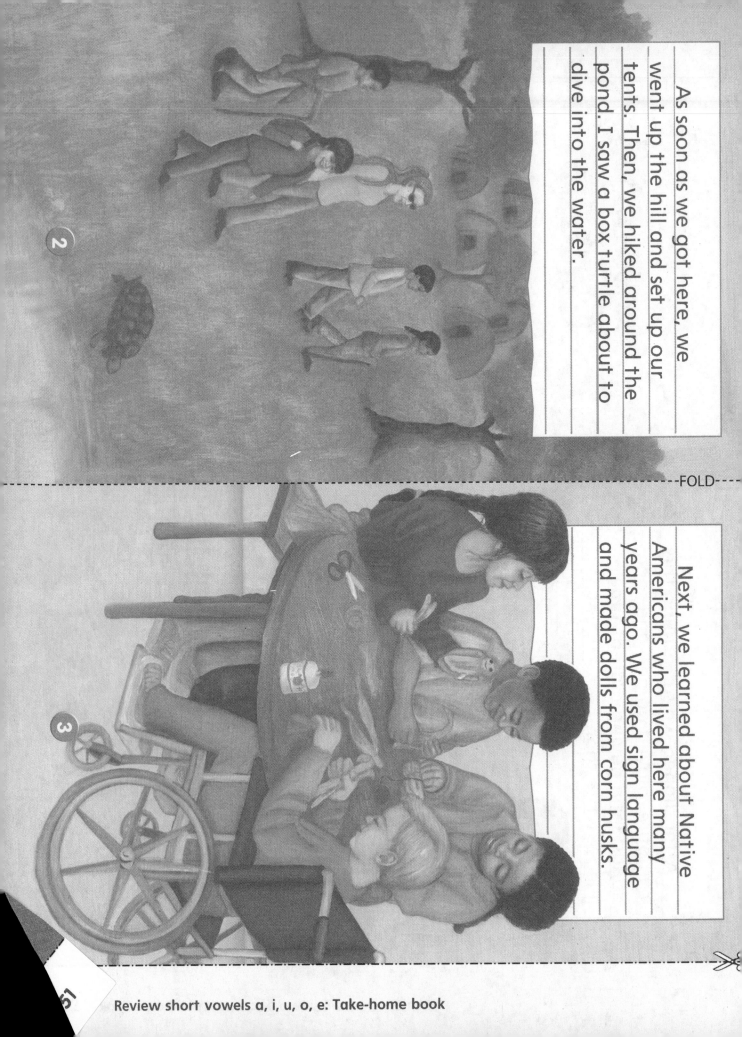

As soon as we got here, we went up the hill and set up our tents. Then, we hiked around the pond. I saw a box turtle about to dive into the water.

2

Next, we learned about Native Americans who lived here many years ago. We used sign language and made dolls from corn husks.

3

Review short vowels a, i, u, o, e: Take-home book

Name _____

Copyright © Savvas Learning Company LLC. All Rights Reserved.

▶ **Fill in** the name of each picture.

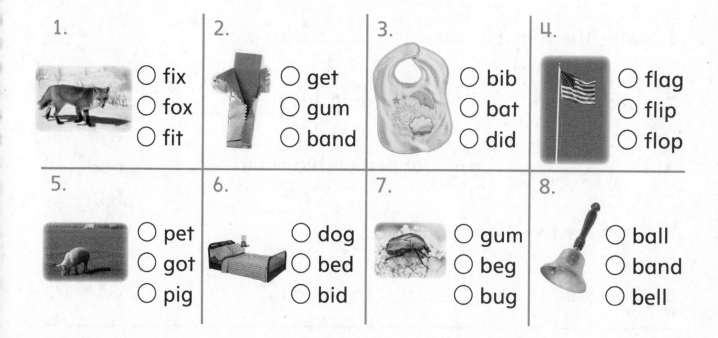

1.
○ fix
○ fox
○ fit

2.
○ get
○ gum
○ band

3.
○ bib
○ bat
○ did

4.
○ flag
○ flip
○ flop

5.
○ pet
○ got
○ pig

6.
○ dog
○ bed
○ bid

7.
○ gum
○ beg
○ bug

8.
○ ball
○ band
○ bell

▶ **Say** the name of each picture. **Fill in** the bubble beside the letter that stands for the short vowel sound.

9.
○ a
○ e
○ i

10.
○ e
○ u
○ i

11.
○ i
○ e
○ a

12.
○ o
○ u
○ e

13.
○ o
○ i
○ u

14.
○ e
○ i
○ o

15.
○ a
○ i
○ e

16.
○ a
○ e
○ i

Short vowels: Assessment

Find the word in the box that will finish each sentence. Print the word on the line.

1. After the rain, I _____ out to play.

2. I slid in the _____ mud.

3. I _____ and landed with a thud!

4. Then, I was covered with _____.

5. Mom said I _____ to come in.

ran
mud
wet
had
fell

6. I got mud on the _____.

7. Mom was not _____.

8. She made me _____ in the tub.

9. Then, she gave me a glass of _____.

hop
mad
milk
rug

Can you read each word? Put a ✔ in the box if you can.

☐ does   ☐ about   ☐ our   ☐ other   ☐ then   ☐ where
☐ would ☐ care   ☐ because ☐ under ☐ sure   ☐ good

Short vowel and high-frequency words: Assessment

Read Aloud

Taking Off

Mary McB. Green

The airplane taxis down the field
It lifts its wheels above the ground,
It skims above the trees,
It rises higher and higher
Away up toward the sun,
It's just a speck against the sky
—And now it's gone!

TALK About It How would you travel to faraway places?

Dear Family,

As we explore different ways of traveling and places to visit, your child will be learning long vowel sounds in words such as boat, jeep, bike, plane, and mule. Here are some activities you and your child can do together to practice long vowel sounds.

▶ Read a travel article, advertisement, or brochure about a place you would like to visit. Help your child find words with long vowel sounds.

▶ Ask your child to write about a trip he or she would like to take. Talk about the story, and then take turns pointing to all the words with long vowel sounds.

▶ You and your child might enjoy reading these books together.

Axle Annie by Robin Pulver
Iron Horses by Verla Kay

Sincerely,

_____

Estimada familia:

A medida que exploremos las diferentes formas de viajar y los lugares a visitar, su hijo/a aprenderá las vocales de sonidos largos en inglés, tales como boat (barco), jeep (yip), bike (bicicleta), plane (avión) y mule (mula). Aquí tienen algunas actividades que pueden hacer juntos para practicar las vocales de sonidos largos.

▶ Lean un artículo, un anuncio o un volante de viajes acerca de un lugar que les gustaría visitar. Ayuden a su hijo/a a encontrar palabras con vocales de sonidos largos.

▶ Pídanle a su hijo/a que escriba acerca de un viaje que le gustaría dar.

Hablen acerca de lo que escribió y tomen turno para señalar todas las palabras que contienen vocales de sonidos largos.

▶ Ustedes y su hijo/a disfrutarán leyendo estos libros juntos.

Axle Annie de Robin Pulver
Iron Horses de Verla Kay

Sinceramente,

_____

Copyright © Savvas Learning Company LLC. All Rights Reserved.

Name_____

I made a small, gray boat today.
I shaped it from some clay.
Let's take it to the clear, blue bay
And watch it sail away.

▶ **Find the word that will finish each sentence. Print it on the line.**

> **RULE**
> If a syllable or one-syllable word has two vowels, the first vowel usually stands for the long sound, and the second vowel is silent as in **made**, **bay**, and **sail**. The letters **a_e**, **ai**, and **ay** can stand for the long **a** sound.

1. Jane made a _____ when she saw the rain.

2. She wanted the rain to go _____.

3. She had planned to _____ outside.

4. Then, Jake _____ over.

5. Jake and Jane played _____ inside.

away
face
games
came
play

6. The children had to _____ for the rain to stop.

7. Jane's mom baked a _____.

8. Jane and Jake _____ a piece.

9. At last, the _____ stopped.

rain
ate
wait
cake

TALK About It What could Jane and Jake do outside?

Long vowel a: High-frequency words, critical thinking   **57**

Copyright © Savvas Learning Company LLC. All Rights Reserved.

Circle each long a word in the box.
Then, print the name of each picture on the line.

tap	tape	cap	cape	at	ate
pail	mat	rain	gate	hay	ham

1.
2.
3.
4.

cape   pail   rain   hay

Circle the word that will finish each sentence. Print it on the line.

5. It is a nice _day_ today.   day   rain   rake

6. May we go to the _take_?   bake   take   lake

7. Let's _take_ a picnic lunch.   mail   take   say

8. We can bring a _____ and shovel.   pail   mail   rain

9. We could _____ sand castles.   make   wake   fake

10. Our dog _____ could come with us.   take   Jake   save

11. Is there any _____ we can go today?   say   tail   way

58 Long vowel a: Sound to symbol, high-frequency words

HOME With your child, take turns writing long *a* words by changing the *m* in *make* and the *d* in *day*.

Name _____

Your kite rises high
In the wide, blue sky.
It's nothing like mine,
Which is stuck in that pine.

▶ Circle **the name of each picture.**

RULE

If a syllable or one-syllable word has two vowels, the first vowel usually stands for the long sound, and the second vowel is silent as in **kite** and **pine**. The letters **i_e** and **ie** can stand for the long **i** sound.

1.

dim   dime

2.

pig   pile

3.

bike   bib

4.

bib   bite

▶ Circle **the word that will finish each sentence. Then, print it on the line.**

5. Mike likes to ride a _____ .   bit   bike   bite

6. Diane likes to _____ .   hike   hill   him

7. Ike likes cherry _____ .   pie   pig   pine

8. Kyle likes to fly a _____ .   bite   hive   kite

9. Fido likes to _____ .   rid   hide   hive

10. I like to laugh and _____ .   tide   smile   tip

Copyright © Savvas Learning Company LLC. All Rights Reserved.

▶ **Circle the word that will finish each sentence. Print it on the line.**

1. A turtle can _____ inside its shell.   dime   time   hide

2. _____ can hide in a nest very well.   Mice   tile   pie

3. My dog can hide behind our _____.   likes   bikes   dives

4. A bee can hide in its _____.   hive   time   kite

5. A spider can hide anywhere it _____.   pine   mine   likes

6. I _____ to hide things here and there.   like   mile   dime

7. No one can find _____ at bedtime.   dime   Mike   tries

▶ **Circle each long i word in the box.**
Print the name of each picture on the line.

dim	dime	pin	pine	rid	ride
mine	tie	sit	kite	nine	line

8.

9.

10.

11.

Long vowel i: Sound to symbol, high-frequency words

HOME Ask your child to think of a word that rhymes with each of the picture names above.

Name_____

> **Read the words in the box. Write a word to finish each sentence.**

| could |
| over |
| very |
| come |
| One |
| these |

1. _____ day, Mom and I drove to Lake Baker.

2. We asked Jane to _____ with us.

3. Mom told Jane she _____ bring her dog Ike.

4. We went _____ a bridge to get to the lake.

5. The lake was _____ blue.

6. We drew _____ pictures of our day.

Copyright © Savvas Learning Company LLC. All Rights Reserved.

▶ Unscramble **the letters to write the words. The shapes will help you** print **the words.**

1. vero

2. ervy

3. ldcou

4. ethse

5. moce

6. neo

CHECKING UP

▶ Put a ✔ next to each word you can read.

☐ come ☐ very ☐ one ☐ these ☐ could ☐ over

HOME

Help your child make up a sentence for each high-frequency word, such as *These books are heavy.*

Name_____

Sue's old blue truck has bells.
It plays some jolly tunes.
Sue loves the way it sounds,
But not its smelly fumes!

► Circle yes **or** no **to answer each sentence. Then** circle **the long u word in each sentence.** Print **it on the line.**

RULE

If a syllable or one-syllable word has two vowels, the first vowel usually stands for the long sound, and the second vowel is silent as in **Sue**, **blue**, and **fumes**. The letters **u_e**, **ui**, and **ue** can stand for the long **u** sound.

1. A red vase is blue.   _____   yes   no

2. We can get toothpaste in a tube.   _____   yes   no

3. A baby lion is a cube.   _____   yes   no

4. A mule has nine tails.   _____   yes   no

5. You stick things together with glue.   _____   yes   no

6. We can eat a suit.   _____   yes   no

7. A rule is a pet that can sing.   _____   yes   no

8. We play a song with a flute.   _____   yes   no

9. We can hum a tune.   _____   yes   no

Copyright © Savvas Learning Company LLC. All Rights Reserved.

► Read **the words in the box. Print the short u words in the ducks' pond.**
Print the long u words in the mule's pen.

bug	jump	suit	tune	bump	tube
dug	glue	nut	rule	music	hum
	luck	jug	blue	flute	

short

long

HOME Ask your child to suggest three short *u* words and three long *u* words to add to the lists.

Name_____

> Read **each word**. If the word has a long vowel, fill in the bubble in front of long. If the word has a short vowel, fill in the bubble in front of short.

1. late ○ long ○ short

2. June ○ long ○ short

3. mule ○ long ○ short

4. man ○ long ○ short

5. tube ○ long ○ short

6. ride ○ long ○ short

7. rain ○ long ○ short

8. pick ○ long ○ short

9. six ○ long ○ short

10. use ○ long ○ short

11. cute ○ long ○ short

12. cap ○ long ○ short

13. bat ○ long ○ short

14. time ○ long ○ short

15. fun ○ long ○ short

16. bake ○ long ○ short

17. lick ○ long ○ short

18. us ○ long ○ short

19. map ○ long ○ short

20. wide ○ long ○ short

21. gate ○ long ○ short

22. wipe ○ long ○ short

23. pie ○ long ○ short

24. tune ○ long ○ short

Copyright © Savvas Learning Company LLC. All Rights Reserved.

> Circle **the word that will finish each sentence.** Print **it on the line.**

1. We _____ to play music.   ride   like   hike

2. It is a nice _____ to spend a day.   pay   side   way

3. June likes to play her _____.   flute   suit   time

4. Jay can play his _____.   bake   tuba   tub

5. Mike _____ tunes on his bugle.   side   skit   plays

6. _____ plays a bugle, too.   Sue   suit   like

7. _____ like to play my drum.   It   I   Ice

8. We all sing _____.   tunes   times   tiles

9. We can play _____ in a parade.   music   suit   fan

10. Will our uniforms come on _____?   tip   cub   time

11. We play at football _____, too!   gum   games   gate

 What kind of group do the children belong to?

 Ask your child to group the words he or she wrote according to the vowel sounds.

Name _____

Phonics & Reading

The Race

A tortoise named Sue and a hare named Jake met one day. Jake said, "Let's race. You make the rules."

Sue said, "Fine. I will ride my old blue bike. You can use your skates."

They took off side by side, but Jake was much faster. "I am way ahead. I will take a nap by the side of the path," he said.

Soon, Jake woke up. He began to skate, but it was too late! Sue waved from the finish line. She had stayed on her bike, and she had won the race.

1. Sue and Jake had a _____.

2. Sue rode an old _____ bike, and Jake used _____.

3. Sue waved at Jake from the finish _____.

TALK About It
Why do you think Sue won the race?

Copyright © Savvas Learning Company LLC. All Rights Reserved.

Use long **a**, **i**, and **u** words to finish each word ladder. Change only one letter in each word.

1. Begin with **cute**.
   End with **tune**.

   cute

   cube

   tube

   tune

2. Go from **five** to **lone**.

   five

3. Go from **base** to **hike**.

   base

4. Go from **June** to **cave**.

   June

HOME

Have your child make up a sentence for each word in one word ladder, such as *A kitten is soft and cute.*

Name_____

I know a silly mole
In a yellow overcoat.
He rows down the coast
In a little silver boat.

I hope to go with Mole
To places near and far.
If we can't go by boat,
Then we'll go by car.

▶ **Find the word in the box that will finish each sentence. Print it on the line.**

RULE

If a syllable or one-syllable word has two vowels, the first vowel usually stands for the long sound, and the second vowel is silent as in **mole** and **boat**. The letters **o_e**, **ow**, **oe**, and **oa** can all stand for the long **o** sound.

1. Rover poked his _____ into his bowl.

2. He hoped to find a _____ .

3. There was no bone in his _____ .

4. Then, along came his _____ , Joe.

5. Something was in the pocket of Joe's _____ .

6. Joe said, "I have something to _____ you."

7. Oh, boy! It was a bone for _____

coat
owner
Rover
show
bowl
bone
nose

 What do dogs like to do with bones?

Copyright © Savvas Learning Company LLC. All Rights Reserved.

Long vowel o: High-frequency words, critical thinking   **69**

▶ **Circle the name of each picture.**

1. cot   coat

2. road   rod

3. got   goat

4. note   not

5. sap   soap

6. rope   rot

▶ Say the word in the box. Then read the sentence. To finish the sentence, think of a word that rhymes with the word in the box. Print the word on the line.

7. Joe was taking a ride in his _____.

8. Joe's dog Rover wanted to _____, too.

9. Rover poked Joe with his _____.

10. Joe told Rover to _____ into the boat.

11. Then, Joe untied the _____.

12. Finally, Joe began to _____.

| coat |
| no |
| rose |
| top |
| hope |
| mow |

70 Long vowel o: Picture-text match high-frequency words

HOME

Ask your child to spell the words he or she wrote.

Name _____

▶ **Print** the name of each picture on the line.

1.

sodp

2.

tail

3.

kite

4.

rodd

5.
toothpst

6.

swim

▶ **What would you pack if you were taking a trip?** Choose a word from the word box that rhymes and print it on the line.

7. Very nice! Pack some toy ___ mice ___ .

8. Oh, my! Don't forget your ___ suit ___ .

9. How cute! Take your bathing ___ rate ___ .

10. For goodness' sake! Bring a little ___ tie ___ .

> tie
> mice
> suit
> rake

Copyright © Savvas Learning Company LLC. All Rights Reserved.

Review long vowels a, i, u, o: Rhyme **71**

Fill in the bubble in front of the word that will finish each sentence. Print the word on the line.

1. Tim had a nice _____ outside. ○ Tim ○ time

2. He _____ his bike. ○ rode ○ rod

3. He flew his _____ with June. ○ kite ○ kit

4. He played _____ and seek. ○ hid ○ hide

5. Then, _____ and June came inside. ○ Tim ○ time

6. They _____ some cookies. ○ mad ○ made

7. They _____ every bite. ○ ate ○ at

8. "Let's make ice _____," said June. ○ cubes ○ cub

9. "We can _____ grape juice." ○ us ○ use

10. Next, Tim made a paper _____. ○ plan ○ plane

11. June made a paper _____. ○ hate ○ hat

12. Tim said, "I _____ you had fun." ○ hope ○ hop

 Do you think Tim and June had fun? Why or why not?

HOME Have your child read the sentences and identify each word with a long vowel sound such as *nice* and *bike*.

72 Review long vowels a, i, u, o: High-frequency words, critical thinking

Name_____

Meet Neal the Seal
Who moves on wheels.
He drives a green jeep
And makes the horn beep.

► Circle **the name of each picture.**

RULE
If a syllable or one-syllable word has two vowels, the first vowel usually stands for the long sound, and the second vowel is silent. You can hear the long **e** sound in **seal** and **jeep**. The letters **ea** and **ee** can stand for the long **e** sound.

1. set
   seal
   seed

2. feel
   fell
   feet

3. jays
   jeans
   jeeps

4. bet
   bee
   beat

5. beets
   beds
   beads

6. jet
   jeep
   Jean

► Circle **the word that will finish each sentence.** Underline **the letters in the word that stand for the long e sound. Then** print **the word on the line.**

7. Seals live in the _____.   seat   sea   set

8. They _____ fish.   neat   eat   feet

9. We can teach _____ tricks.   east   seals   beets

10. Have you _____ a seal show?   set   free   seen

11. We will see one next _____.   week   met   beak

Copyright © Savvas Learning Company LLC. All Rights Reserved.

Circle **the long e words in the puzzle.**

k	f	s	r	j
s	e	e	n	e
a	e	a	o	a
s	t	t	p	n
p	e	a	b	s

jeans
feet
pea
seat
seen

▶ Write **the word from the box that will finish each sentence.**

1. I wore my new blue _____ to the zoo.

2. I sat on a _____ that had gum on it.

3. I spilled _____ soup on my jeans.

4. Mud from my _____ splashed on them.

5. I've never _____ such a big mess.

74 **Long vowel e: Words in context**

HOME

Help your child make up a new story
using the long e words in the word box.

Name _____

> **Say** the name of each picture. **Print** the vowel you hear on the first line. If the vowel is short, **print** an **S** on the second line. If the vowel is long, **print** an **L** on the second line.

1.

_____ _____

2.

_____ _____

3.

_____ _____

4.

_____ _____

5.

_____ _____

6.

_____ _____

7.

_____ _____

8.

_____ _____

9.

_____ _____

10.

_____ _____

11.

_____ _____

12.

_____ _____

> **Finish** the rhyming words.

13. hat   mat sat

14. went   d   r

15. fun   r   b

16. gate   l   d

17. like   b   h

18. goat   c   b

Copyright © Savvas Learning Company LLC. All Rights Reserved.

Change **the first vowel in each word to another vowel. Write the new word.**

1. boat _____

2. oar _____

3. cone _____

4. nip _____

5. sod _____

6. hop _____

7. wide _____

8. tame _____

9. red _____

10. ran _____

11. bake _____

12. map _____

 Find a word in the box that rhymes with each word. Print it on the line.

13. time _____

14. cube _____

15. rub _____

16. need _____

17. tape _____

18. bat _____

19. clue _____

> tube
> cub
> blue
> cape
> dime
> hat
> feed

20. seat _____

21. fin _____

22. hope _____

23. bet _____

24. rob _____

25. toad _____

26. fine _____

> tin
> road
> cob
> mine
> rope
> get
> heat

HOME Ask your child to read the rhyming words and tell whether each pair has a long or short vowel sound.

Name _____

> Read the words in the box. Write a word to
> finish each sentence.

song	boy
said	girl
something	people

1. We met many _____ at the bus stop.

2. Steve _____ , "We will have to wait."

3. "Let us do _____ until the bus comes," I said.

4. One _____ read to us from her book.

5. One _____ sang to us.

6. Then, we all sang a _____ .

Copyright © Savvas Learning Company LLC. All Rights Reserved.

▶ Unscramble **the letters to write the words. The shapes will help you** print **the words.**

1. peolep

2. lirg

3. oyb

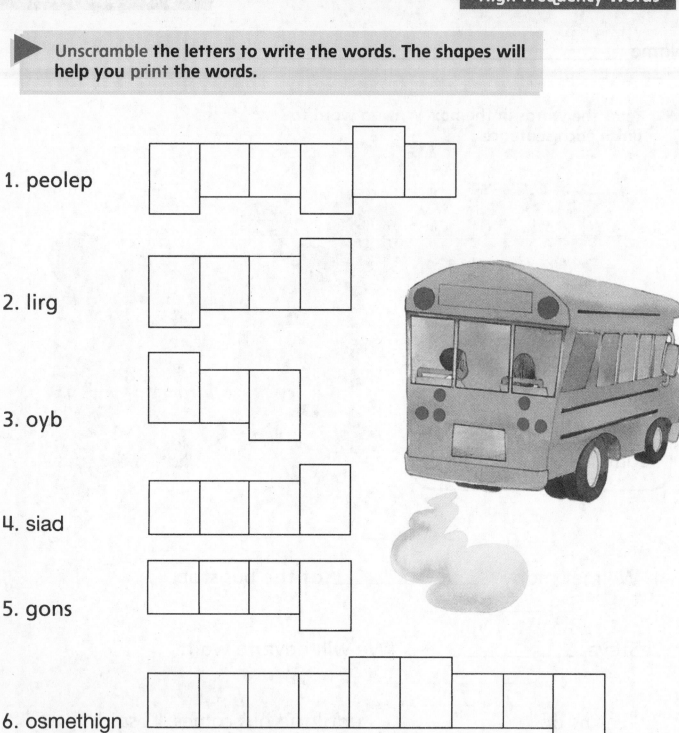

4. siad

5. gons

6. osmethign

CHECKING UP

▶ Put a ✔ next to each word you can read.

☐ girl ☐ said ☐ song ☐ something ☐ boy ☐ people

HOME
With your child, make up a sentence for each word.

Name _____

Phonics & Spelling

Say and spell each long vowel word. Print the word in the box that shows its long vowel sound.

use	heel	hay	nine	note
coat	tube	dime	rule	bead
cape	tie	seen	mail	row

Long a			
Long i			
Long o			
Long u			
Long e			

Copyright © Savvas Learning Company LLC. All Rights Reserved.

When you **describe a place**, you tell how it looks. You may tell about colors, shapes, things you see, and sounds. You may say how a place feels such as *hot* or *cold*.

Think about a place you have visited. It can be a place in your town, or faraway. Use sentences to describe this place. Tell how you felt when you visited this place. Some of the words in the word box may help you.

blue	boat	hay	hole	seat
mail	jeans	hope	train	row
bike	ride	use	time	rain

Name the place in the first sentence.

Use colorful words to tell how the place looks.

HOME Help your child think of a title for his or her story.

Copyright © Savvas Learning Company LLC. All Rights Reserved.

Name _____

A Day at the Grand Canyon

Imagine you could take a trip and visit the Grand Canyon. What would you see? How would you spend your day?

1

There are many ways to see the canyon. Some people ride bikes. Some people take buses along roads at the top of the canyon. Some hike the steep trails, and others ride mules. Which way would you like best?

4

FOLD

You would see that the canyon is very wide and deep. In some places, it is up to 18 miles wide and more than a mile deep.

2

You would see walls of rock rise from below. The rock has stripes of color. It looks like a rainbow with many shades of red and brown.

3

UNIT 4

Compounds, Words with le,
Hard and Soft c and g,
Blends, Digraphs, Y as a
Vowel, R-controlled Vowels
Theme: The World Outside

Read Aloud

Earth's Oldest Living Thing

How old is old? Bristlecone pine trees may be the oldest living things on earth. The oldest known bristlecone is almost 5,000 years old.

How do people know how old bristlecone pines are? Scientists study a piece of a tree and count the rings. There is one ring for every year the tree is alive. A thin ring means the year was dry. A thick ring shows good rainfall.

The oldest bristlecone pine trees are found in California. Their secret to a long life is to grow very slowly.

TALK About It

How could the tree rings tell a story about weather over a long time?

Dear Family,

In this unit "The World Outside," your child will learn about compound words (scarecrow), words ending in **le** (candle), hard and soft **c** and **g** (camp, city, go, giant) consonant blends (grapes, plants), digraphs (peach, shell, wheat), **y** as a vowel (baby, try), and r-controlled vowels (barn, fern, bird, corn, fur).

As your child becomes familiar with these words and sounds, you might try these activities together.

▶ With your child, read the selection on page 85. Then, ask your child to find the words with consonant blends such as tree and grow.

watermelon
tomatoes
corn
blueberries
beans
peppers

▶ Help your child plant a lima bean in a paper cup. Talk about what seeds need to grow. Then, have your child make a list of fruits and vegetables that he or she would like to grow in a garden and circle the words with r-controlled vowels.

▶ You and your child might enjoy reading these books together.

The Pumpkin Patch
by Elizabeth King

A Farm of Her Own
by Natalie Kinsey-Warnock

Sincerely,

Estimada familia:

En esta unidad, titulada "El mundo a nuestro alrededor" ("The World Outside"), su hijo/a aprenderá palabras compuestas (scarecrow/ espantapájaros), palabras que terminan en **le** (candle/vela), la **c** y la **g** suave y dura (camp/ campamento, city/ciudad, go/ir, giant/gigante), combinaciones de consonantes (grapes/uvas, plants/plantas), digramas (peach/pera, shell/ concha, wheat/trigo), **y** como una vocal (baby/bebé, try/tratar) y combinaciones de vocales y r (barn/granero, fern/helecho, bird/pájaro, corn/maíz, fur/pelambre).

A medida que su hijo/a se vaya familiarizando con estas palabras y sonidos, pueden hacer las siguientes actividades juntos.

▶ Lean con su hijo/a la selección en la página 85. Después, ayuden a su hijo/a a hallar las palabras con combinaciones de consonantes, como tree (árbol) y grow (crecer).

▶ Si es posible, ayuden a su hijo/a a sembrar una planta de frijoles, por ejemplo habas, en un vaso de papel. Conversen sobre lo que necesitan las semillas para crecer. Luego, pidan a su hijo/a que haga una lista de las frutas y vegetales que le gustaría sembrar en un huerto y, entonces, encierren en un círculo las palabras con combinaciones de vocales y r.

▶ Ustedes y su hijo/a disfrutarán leyendo estos libros juntos.

The Pumpkin Patch de Elizabeth King

A Farm of Her Own de Natalie Kinsey-Warnock

Sinceramente,

Copyright © Savvas Learning Company LLC. All Rights Reserved.

Name _____

Farmer Janet picked an onion,
She picked a turnip and carrots, too.
Janet took them to her kitchen,
There she made a tasty stew.

> Say **the name of each picture.** Circle **each vowel you hear.** Print **the number of syllables you hear on the line.**

RULE

Many words are made of small parts called syllables. Each syllable has one vowel sound.

p(i)cks = 1 syllable
c(a)rr(o)ts = 2 syllables

1. b(a)sk(e)t _2_

2. m(i)tt(e)ns _2_

3. steps _1_

4. p(e)ncil _1_

5. t(e)nt _1_

6. p(u)pp(e)t _2_

7. tr(u)nk _1_

8. r(o)b(o)t _2_

9. p(i)ll(o)w _2_

10. k(i)tt(e)n _2_

11. tr(a)y _1_

12. l(e)m(o)n _1_

**Find the word in the box that names each picture.
Print it on the line to finish the sentence.**

| ribbon | basket | button | pillow |
| kitten | boxes | seven | baby |

1. Molly got a tiny __kitten__ named Popcorn.

2. She tied a blue __ribbon__ on Popcorn.

3. Popcorn was only __seven__ weeks old.

4. She had a nose like a __button__.

5. She liked to play inside __boxes__.

6. Molly made a bed for Popcorn in a __basket__.

7. She put a __pillow__ in the bed to make it soft.

8. Popcorn was like a little __baby__.

 TALK About It **What makes Popcorn like a baby?**

 HOME Say one- and two-syllable words and have your child identify the number of syllables in each word.

Two-syllable words: High-frequency words, critical thinking

Name _____

Pick a bag of apples.
Pick a basket of cucumbers, too.
There's applesauce on the table,
And a dill pickle just for you.

► **Find** the name of each picture in the box. **Print** it on the line.

apple	eagle	people
candle	buckle	whistle
turtle	bottle	table

1.

_____

2.

_____

3.

_____

4.

_____

5.

_____

6.

_____

7.

_____

8.

_____

9.

_____

**Find the word that will finish each sentence.
Print it on the line.**

1. A _____ uses its own shell for a house.

2. It can swim in a pond or a _____.

3. It can _____ around in the water.

4. It climbs on _____ and rocks.

5. An _____ might fly over and scare it.

6. Sometimes, _____ may scare it, too.

7. Then, the turtle can _____ safely
   in its shell.

| pebbles |
| eagle |
| people |
| turtle |
| huddle |
| puddle |
| paddle |

1. My _____ took me to the zoo.

2. Many _____ watched the turtles.

3. We saw _____ turtles hatching
   from their eggs.

4. They were not even as big as a small,
   green _____.

5. As they came out of their shells, they
   began to _____.

6. The zookeeper placed them on a _____.

7. I started to laugh and _____
   when they tried to huddle together.

| giggle |
| table |
| little |
| wiggle |
| pickle |
| people |
| uncle |

 **Where do the turtles
in the stories live?**

 Help your child make up sentences
using some of the words in the boxes.

Words ending in le: High-frequency words, critical thinking

Name_____

Sugar and Spice are Lucy's pet mice.
They are cute and very nice.
Sugar nibbles a slice of cheese,
Spice snacks on carrots and on peas.

▶ Say **the name of each picture. If it has a soft c sound,** circle **the picture. If it has a hard c sound,** draw a line **under it.**

> **RULE**
> When **c** is followed by **e, i,** or **y,** it usually has a soft sound. You can hear the soft **c** sound in **mice.**

1.

face

2.

cap

3.

clock

4.

cup

5.

pencil

6.

cake

7.

mice

8.

ice

9.

celery

Copyright © Savvas Learning Company LLC. All Rights Reserved.

► **Circle** the word that will finish each sentence. **Print** it on the line.

	can	cage
	cape	came

1. Cindy and Vince _____ run fast.

	mice	race
	nice	next

2. They will run in a _____ at school.

	cap	cane
	come	cat

3. The kids _____ to watch.

	nice	rice
	place	slice

4. Cindy hopes to win first _____.

	rice	nice
	laces	price

5. The _____ of their shoes are tied.

	next	nice
	fence	can

6. They race past the _____.

	mice	cereal
	nice	price

7. It's a tie. They win _____ prizes.

	clue	cats
	case	class

8. The _____ cheers for them.

	lace	faces
	race	space

9. Cindy and Vince have smiling _____.

	cones	cape
	mice	nice

10. The kids get ice-cream _____.

 Do Cindy and Vince enjoy racing? How do you know?

 Help your child group all the hard c words and all the soft c words.

Hard and soft c: High-frequency words, critical thinking

Name _____

Gentle giraffes,
Gaze through the trees.
Bigger than giants,
They nibble the leaves.

Say the name of each picture. If the name has a **soft g sound,** circle the picture. If it has a **hard g sound,** draw a line **under it.**

RULE

When **g** is followed by **e, i,** or **y,** it usually has a soft sound. You can hear the soft **g** sound in **giraffe.**

1.

game

2.

gym

3.

goat

4.

page

5.

giant

6.

gum

7.

dragon

8.

egg

9.

giraffe

Copyright © Savvas Learning Company LLC. All Rights Reserved.

The letter **g** can make a hard or a soft sound. Read the words in the box. Listen for the sounds of **g**. Print the words under Soft **g** Words or Hard **g** Words.

gift	gem	age	dog	cage	large	good	gum
huge	gave	goat	stage	wag	page	wage	gold
gym	gate	giant	gentle	egg	game	giraffe	give

Soft g Words　　　　　　　　**Hard g Words**

_____　　　_____

_____　　　_____

_____　　　_____

_____　　　_____

_____　　　_____

_____　　　_____

_____　　　_____

_____　　　_____

_____　　　_____

_____　　　_____

HOME Say a word from the box. Ask your child to spell it and tell if the word has a soft or hard *g* sound.

Name_____

> Complete each sentence with one of the words in the box. Write the word on the line. One word is used more than once.

> only   laugh   own
>
> even   their   might

1. Jill and Sam took _____ little sister Bea to the fair.

2. Sam was the _____ one who wanted to milk a cow.

3. Jill said the petting zoo _____ be fun for Bea.

4. Bea liked the piglets _____ better than the lambs.

5. The silly clowns made them all _____.

6. Jill got some popcorn to share, but Sam wanted his

   _____ box of popcorn.

7. Bea asked Jill and Sam when they _____ come back to the fair.

Copyright © Savvas Learning Company LLC. All Rights Reserved.

▶ **Read the words in the box. Write the word that goes with each clue in the puzzle.**

only	laugh	own
even	their	might

Across

1. When something belongs to you, you _____ it.
2. You do this when you hear a funny joke. _____
3. If a book belongs to Sue and Moe, it is _____ book.

Down

1. If there is no one but you, then you are the _____ one.
4. *Maybe* means you _____ be able to go to a friend's house.
5. This word means the opposite of odd. _____

▶ **Write a sentence using one of the words on this page.**

_____

_____

HOME With your child, make flash cards for the words in this lesson, and have him or her use each word in a sentence.

Name _____

Read the story. Print a word from the story to finish each sentence.

The Giant Giraffe

The giraffe is the tallest animal that can be found anywhere on land. At least three people would have to stand on each other's shoulders to reach a giraffe's forehead. Because it is so tall, it can nibble leaves from treetops.

Although the giraffe has very long legs, it can gallop gracefully. The giraffe is able to race away when it faces danger. When it can not run away, the giraffe will kick with its heavy feet.

The body of a giraffe is covered with large, brown spots. These spots help the giraffe to blend in with the trees and keep it safe from harm.

Copyright © Savvas Learning Company LLC. All Rights Reserved.

1. The _____ is the tallest land animal.

2. At least three _____ would have to stand on each other's shoulders to pet a giraffe.

3. The giraffe is tall enough to nibble leaves

   from _____.

4. With its long legs, it is able to race away

   from _____.

Use **words with le, c, and g** to finish each word ladder. Change **only one letter in each word.**

1. Begin with **gave**.
End with **come**.

_____ gave _____

_____ game _____

_____ came _____

_____ come _____

2. Begin with **tangle**.
End with **jiggle**.

_____

_____

_____

_____

3. Begin with **page**.
End with **rice**.

_____

_____

_____

_____

4. Begin with **cage**.
End with **wigs**.

_____

_____

_____

_____

Compounds; syllables; words with le;
sounds of c, g

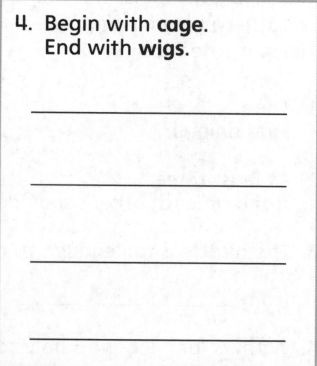

Work with your child to make a
word ladder beginning with *come*
and ending with *long*.

Name _____

Green frogs, tree frogs,
There are so many kinds.
Brown frogs, bullfrogs,
We can't make up our minds.

▶ **Say the name of each picture. Print its beginning blend on the line. Trace the whole word.**

RULE

A **consonant blend** is two or more consonants that come together in a word. Their sounds blend together, but each sound is heard. You can hear **r** blends in **green, tree,** and **frogs.**

1. apes

2. og

3. ee

4. ain

▶ **Use the words above to answer the riddles.**

5. I can jump and hop.
You find me in a pond.
I eat bugs.

I am a _____.

6. I am green.
You can find me in a park.
Birds live in me.

I am a _____.

7. I can be small or big.
I make a good toy.
I run on a track.

I am a _____.

8. We grow on vines.
We come in bunches.
We are good to eat.

We are _____.

▶ **Circle the word that names the picture.**

1. 	2. 	3. 	4. 
grapes	trim	trade	drive
grass	truck	trap	drum
grade	train	tree	drink
5. 	6. 	7. 	8. 
from	train	dress	gray
frost	truck	drapes	grass
fruit	trick	drum	grab

▶ **Find the blend in each word. Circle it. Print it on the line.**

9. b r i n g _____

10. f r y _____

11. t r i p _____

12. g r a d e _____

13. d r i v e _____

14. g r a s s _____

15. b r a v e _____

16. t r i c k _____

17. g r a i n _____

18. b r i d e _____

19. c r u m b _____

20. t r a i n _____

21. c r o s s _____

22. b r i c k _____

23. t r a d e _____

24. f r e e _____

25. p r i c e _____

26. f r u i t _____

 Ask your child to make sentences using two of the picture words such as, *A train is faster than a truck.*

Name _____

The wind blows the clouds.
Sleet turns to snow.
Winter's here again,
And sledding we will go!

▶ Say the name of each picture. Print its beginning blend on the line.

1.  ____	2.  ____	3.  ____
4.  ____	5.  ____	6.  ____

▶ Circle the word that will finish each sentence. Print it on the line.

7. Snow covers the ground like a white

   _____.   cloud   clap

8. The wind _____ the snow around.   blue   blows

9. It covers the trees and _____, too.   plants   plays

10. I like to _____ in the snow.   play   plants

11. I am _____ that it is wintertime.   glad   glass

Copyright © Savvas Learning Company LLC. All Rights Reserved.

> **Print the word on the line that answers each riddle. The pictures will help you.**

1. Sometimes I ring.
Sometimes I chime.
I tick-tock all the
time.

_____

2. High up on a pole I go.
I flap when
breezes begin
to blow.

_____

3. I hold the food
you eat.
Find me under
rice or meat.

_____

4. I make things
stick for you. I
stick to you, too.

_____

> **Find a word in the box to finish each sentence. Print it on the line.**

5. I have a new magnifying _____.

6. When I hold it _____ to things, they get bigger.

7. A blade of _____ looks like a stem.

8. _____ of wood are really full of holes.

9. A _____ looks like a big black monster!

10. A toy _____ looks like a real plane.

Blocks
grass
fly
plane
close
glass

 Ask your child to name other words that begin with cl, fl, pl, and bl, such as *flower* or *cloud*.

Name _____

Said Squiggle Snake to Slimy Snail,
"Let's slide on the slippery trail."
Said Slimy Snail to Squiggle Snake,
"Slow down, for goodness' sake!"

▶ Say the name of each picture. Find its beginning blend in the box. Print it on the line.

RULE

Remember that in a **consonant blend** the sounds of the consonants blend together, and each sound is heard. You can hear **s** blends in **slide, snake,** and **squiggle.**

sc	st	sp	sn	squ	scr	str	sl	sm	sw

1.

2.

3.

4.

5.

6.

7.

8.

9.

10.

11.

12.

Copyright © Savvas Learning Company LLC. All Rights Reserved.

Blends with s   **105**

Find a word in the box to finish each sentence. Print it on the line.

1. Did you ever _____ to think about snakes?

2. Snakes have long, _____ bodies.

3. Snakes can move both fast and _____.

4. _____ have no arms or legs.

5. They still have the _____ to move.

6. Some snakes can even _____.

7. Their _____ looks slimy, but it's dry.

8. Snakes _____ some people, but not me.

scare
slim
skin
stop
skill
Snakes
swim
slow

Circle the name of each picture.

9. 	10. 	11. 
swim stem	scream screen	smile smoke
12. 	13. 	14. 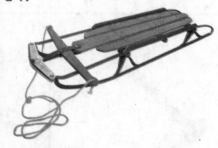
stops steps	snake sneak	sled slide

106   Blends with s: Picture-text match

 Help your child identify the words in the box that have the same beginning sound.

Name _____

A skunk is just outside my tent.
I think I'd best not scare it.
For if it sprays me with its scent,
All week long, I'll wear it.

RULE

Remember that in a **consonant blend** the sounds of the consonants blend together, and each sound is heard. You can hear blends at the end of **swing** and **trunk.**

▶ Circle **the word that answers each riddle.** Print **it on the line.**

1. All mail needs these. What are they?

stamps   stumps

_____

2. We can ride on it. What is it?

string   swing

_____

3. An elephant has one. What is it?

skunk   trunk

_____

4. We can eat it. What is it?

toast   list

_____

5. It hides your face. What is it?

task   mask

_____

6. We can sleep in it. What is it?

tent   plant

_____

7. We have two of these. What are they?

lands   hands

_____

8. Fish swim in it. What is it?

tank   wink

_____

9. It can float. What is it?

raft   left

_____

Copyright © Savvas Learning Company LLC. All Rights Reserved.

Final blends   **107**

▶ **Find** the word in the box that names each picture. **Print** it on the line.

milk	skunk	tent	belt	trunk	plants
nest	ring	stamp	raft	desk	mask

1.

_____

2.

_____

3.

_____

4.

_____

5.

_____

6.

_____

7.

_____

8.

_____

9.

_____

10.

_____

11.

_____

12.

_____

108 Final blends

Ask your child to name other words that end with *ng*, *sk*, and *mp*, such as *sing* and *camp*.

Name _____

Phonics & Reading

Read **the story.** Use **a word from the story to finish each sentence.** Print **the word on the line.**

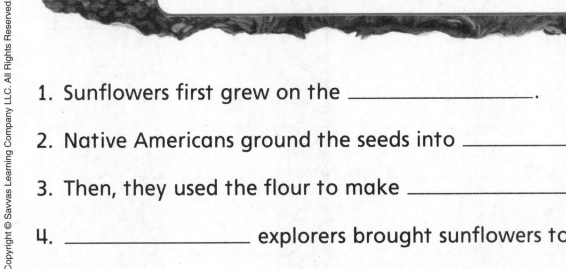

Sunflowers

Wild sunflowers first grew on the plains in the West. Native Americans roasted the seeds and ground them into flour for bread. We still eat sunflower seeds. They are a great food for birds and people.

Spanish explorers brought sunflower plants back to Europe. Now, sunflowers grow all over the world. Sunflowers grow in many different sizes. The smallest are only one or two feet tall. The biggest plants are twelve feet tall!

1. Sunflowers first grew on the _____.

2. Native Americans ground the seeds into _____.

3. Then, they used the flour to make _____.

4. _____ explorers brought sunflowers to Europe.

TALK About It Why do you think Spanish explorers brought sunflowers back to Europe?

Review r, l, s blends: Reading; critical thinking   **109**

Copyright © Savvas Learning Company LLC. All Rights Reserved.

Use **beginning or ending blends to finish each word ladder. Change only one letter at a time.**

1. Go from **harp** to **band**.

harp

hard

hand

band

2. Go from **song** to **silk**.

song

siny

sink

silk

3. Go from **clips** to **glass**.

clips

clides

clas

flass

4. Go from **spell** to **stall**.

spell

spill

still

stall

HOME

Using one of the words he or she formed, work with your child to make a word ladder of four words.

Name _____

Baby bird, are you ready?
Baby bird, can you try?
Spread your tiny wings,
For now it is time to fly!

▶ Circle **each word in which y has a
long e sound.**

RULE
Sometimes **y** can stand for the vowel
sound of long **e** or long **i.** You can hear
the long **e** sound in **baby.**

1. baby
2. cry
3. happy
4. why

5. try
6. every
7. hurry
8. ti...

9. Molly
10. sandy
11. shy
12. puppy

13. penny
14. Freddy
15. funny
16. bunny

▶ Circle **the words in the sentences in which y has a long e sound.**

17. Ty and Molly were helping take care of baby Freddy.

18. They heard Freddy cry in his crib.

19. They went to help in a hurry.

20. They had to try everything to make him happy.

21. Ty read him a funny book about fish that fly.

22. Molly gave him her bunny to play with.

23. Ty made very silly faces.

24. Finally, Freddy was happy.

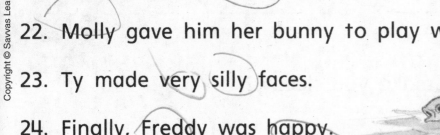

Copyright © Savvas Learning Company LLC. All Rights Reserved.

Vowel sounds of y: Words in context **111**

> **Circle each word with a y that sounds like long i.**

RULE

When **y** is the only vowel at the end of a one-syllable word, **y** usually has the long **i** sound. You can hear the long **i** sound in **try**.

1. try
2. Freddy
3. sly
4. buggy
5. funny

6. bunny
7. dry
8. silly
9. rocky
10. my

11. Ty
12. windy
13. by
14. sky
15. sunny

16. sleepy
17. fly
18. happy
19. muddy
20. cry

21. sneaky
22. lucky
23. shy
24. puppy
25. Molly

26. why
27. jolly
28. baby
29. fry
30. very

> **Circle each word with y that sounds like long i in the sentences.**

31. Why do onions make us cry when we are happy?

32. Why is the sky blue on a sunny day?

33. Why do bats fly at night?

34. Why is a desert dry and a swamp muddy?

35. Why can a bird fly but not a puppy?

36. Why do we look silly if we try to fly?

37. Why is a fox sneaky and sly?

38. Why is a bunny shy?

39. Why does a rainy sky make you sleepy?

40. Do you ever wonder why?

Ask your child to use three of the circled words on this page in a sentence.

Name _____

> Read the word in each paw print. If the y stands for a long i sound, draw a line under the word. If it stands for a long e sound, circle the word.

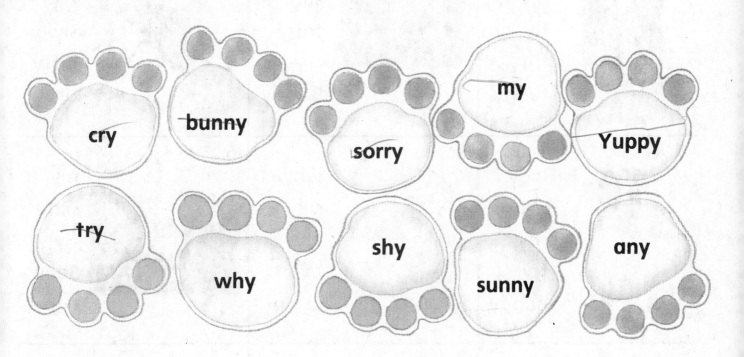

cry

bunny

sorry

my

Yuppy

try

why

shy

sunny

any

> Find a word from the top of the page to finish each sentence. Print it on the line.

1. ___Yuppy___ the puppy was digging a hole

2. Suddenly he heard a ___cry___ from inside.

3. A very angry ___bunny___ popped out of the hole.

4. "Why are you digging up ___My___ happy home?"

5. Yuppy yapped, "Oh, my! I'm very ___sorry___."

6. "I'll ___try___ to help you fix it!"

Copyright © Savvas Learning Company LLC. All Rights Reserved.

Say the name of each picture. Circle each word that has the same sound of **y** as the picture name.

1.

baby
my
fly
(fifty)
(funny)

2.

(sky)
(sunny)
(fairy)
cry
Bobby

3.

dolly
(try)
(sly)
kitty
(dry)

4.

(lady)
(penny)
shy
fry
(happy)

5.

why
(silly)
(lily)
by
(bunny)

6.

(my)
sixty
fly
Sally
(sky)

7.

jelly
Sandy
(my)
(fry)
(cry)

8.

(lucky)
(try)
(fifty)
sky
(puppy)

9.

(berry)
(very)
try
sly
(any)

10.

cry
(lady)
(many)
sky
by

11.

only
(city)
July
spy
(funny)

12.

my
fly
(fifty)
(happy)
(silly)

HOME Help your child find two words that rhyme in each box.

Name _____

Phonics & Spelling

Say the name of each picture. Find the word in the box and spell it. Then, print the word on the line.

ribbon	gym	globe	baby
stamp	peanut	apple	sky
plant	belt	ice	frog

1. apple

2. belt

3. ice

4. baby

5. plant

6. ribbon

7. globe

8. peanut

9. stamp

10. gym

11. frog

12. sky

Compounds; syllables; le; hard and soft c, g; blends; vowel y　　**115**

Phonics & Writing

Use a **letter tile to make a word with y.**
Write **the words you made on the lines.**

cr dr tr br fr   sl sn sh sk sp

cr __y__

1. dry

2. try

3. fry

4. _____

sky

5. shy

6. spy

7. sly

8. _____

▶ **Write two sentences using some of the words you made.**

I am shy I am in the
play.
The sky was nice
and the sun was nice and blue.

HOME

Have your child write two more
sentences using some of the other
words he or she made.

Copyright © Savvas Learning Company LLC. All Rights Reserved.

Name _____

Twin Pets

Cindy and Cathy are twins. They look alike, but Cindy has an extra freckle on her nose. One day Uncle Gary came to visit. He gave the girls their own gerbils. Cindy and Cathy are glad to get the pets.

1

At bedtime their pets are peppy. Uncle Gary tells the twins that gerbils are *nocturnal*. That means they are awake at night and sleep when it is daytime!

4

Cindy names her gerbil George, and Cathy names her gerbil Greg. The gerbils look alike, but Greg has a black spot on its nose. The twins like to cuddle their gerbils and give them carrots to nibble.

2

Cindy and Cathy take good care of their pets. They feed George and Greg and give them clean water to drink. They clean their cage. The twins wonder why their pets huddle together and sleep all day.

3

Compounds; syllables; le; hard and soft c, g; blends; vowel y: Take-home book

Name_____

Shiny, wet shells on the shore,
More shells down the beach,
There's such a lot to choose from!
Why don't we pick one of each?

> **RULE**
> A **consonant digraph** is two consonants that together stand for one sound. You can hear consonant digraphs in **shells, choose, the,** and **why.**

▶ Circle **the word that will finish each sentence. Print it on the line.**

1. I go to the zoo to see the ___chimp___. chop (chimp) check

2. It smiles to show its ___teeth___. then (teeth) these

3. They are big and ___white___. which what (white)

4. It eats bananas by the ___bunch___. (bunch) reach much

5. Once, I saw it eat a ___peach___. that ship (peach)

6. At times it eats from its ___dish___. wish (dish) swish

7. Then, it naps in the ___shade___. fresh shut (shade)

▶ Find **two words from the list above that begin with ch, wh, th, and sh. Print them on the lines beside the correct consonant digraph.**

8. **ch** chimp / imp

9. **th** teeth / eeth

10. **wh** white / ite

11. **sh** shade / hade

Copyright © Savvas Learning Company LLC. All Rights Reserved.

Fill in **the bubble beside the word that will finish each sentence.** Print **it on the line.**

1. Chip and I didn't know _____Where_____ to go.

         ◉ where
         ○ what

2. We decided to go to the mall to _____shop_____.

         ○ chop
         ◉ shop

3. They sell everything _____there_____.

         ○ this
         ◉ there

4. There was so _____ to choose from.

         ○ catch
         ○ much

5. I couldn't decide _____ I wanted most.

         ○ what
         ○ who

6. Then, I saw some model _____ kits.

         ○ shirt
         ○ ship

7. _____ was what I wanted most.

         ○ When
         ○ That

8. I _____ a clipper ship to make.

         ○ chose
         ○ chair

9. _____ chose a spaceship kit.

         ○ Choose
         ○ Chip

10. _____, we had lunch.

         ○ Then
         ○ That

Where do you think Chip bought his model kit?

Say one of the words in the list. Have your child name the other words that begin with the same sound.

Consonant digraphs sh, th, wh, ch: High-frequency words, critical thinking

Name_____

Say the name of each picture. Circle the consonant digraph you hear.

1.	th **(sh)** ck ch wh	2. **(th)** sh ck ch wh	3.	th sh **(ck)** ch wh	4.	th sh ck **(ch)** wh
5.	th **(sh)** ck ch wh	6. **(th)** sh ck ch wh	7.	th **(sh)** ck ch wh	8.	th sh **(ck)** ch wh
9.	th sh ck **(ch)** wh	10.	th sh **(ck)** ch wh	11.	th sh ck ch **(wh)**	12.	**(sh)** ck ch wh
13.	**(th)** sh ck ch wh	14.	th sh ck **(ch)** wh	15.	**(th)** sh ck ch wh	16.	th sh ck ch **(wh)**

Copyright © Savvas Learning Company LLC. All Rights Reserved.

Consonant digraphs sh, th, wh, ch, ck   **121**

Read the words in the box and circle the hidden pictures. Write the words on the lines. Circle the consonant digraph in each word.

whale	wheel	thumb	clock	truck	duck
fish	peach	chair	thimble	shell	shoe

1. _____   2. _____   3. _____

4. _____   5. _____   6. _____

7. _____   8. _____   9. _____

10. _____   11. _____   12. _____

Have your child find the words with the same consonant digraphs.

Name_____

We garden for hours.
We know how to plant seeds.
We kneel to plant flowers.
We kneel to pull weeds.

▶ Read **each sentence. Find the picture it tells about. Write the sentence letter under the picture.**

RULE
You can hear the consonant digraph **kn** in **kneel** and **knees.**

1.

   a. John has a knot in the rope.
   b. I know what is in the box.
   c. Joan turned the knob.

   _____ C

2.

   K

   a. Theo will knock down the pile.
   b. Mom cut it with a knife.
   c. She knocks on the door.

   B

3.

   K

   a. The knight wore armor.
   b. Tad's knee needs a patch.
   c. Grandma likes to knit.

   C

▶ Find **a word in the box that answers each riddle. Print it on the line.**

4. Something that can cut _____ knife

5. Someone who wore armor _____ knight

6. Something you can tie _____ knot

knife
knot
knight

Copyright © Savvas Learning Company LLC. All Rights Reserved.

Circle **the word that will finish each sentence.**
Print **it on the line.**

1. I __Know__ how to do many things.   know   knot

2. I can spread butter with a __Knife__.   knot   knife

3. I can touch my __Knees__ to my chin.   knees   knew

4. I can tie __Knots__.   knots   knits

5. I can turn the _____ of a door.   knee   knob

6. I can read about _____.   know   knights

7. I can _____ a sweater.   knit   knife

8. I've _____ how to do these
   things for a long time.   knit   known

Think **of a word that begins with kn and** rhymes **with
each word.** Print **the word on the line.**

9.	snow	10.	block	11.	wife
__Know__		__Knock__		__Knife__	
12.	blew	13.	see	14.	hot
_____		_____		_____	
15.	own	16.	sit	17.	sob
_____		_____		_____	

Ask your child to make up sentences
using the *kn* words on the page.

Name _____

A busy wren high on a wreath,
Sang to children playing beneath.
They tried to copy the wren's song.
They sang the tune, but got it wrong.

▶ Find **the word in the box that will finish** each sentence. Print **it on the line.**

> **RULE**
> You can hear the consonant digraph **wr** in **wriggles** and **wren.**

wren	wreck	wrap	wrestle	write
wrist	wrench	wrecker	wrong	wriggle

1. To move around is to ___wriggle___.

2. The opposite of **right** is ___wrong___.

3. A small bird is a ___wren___.

4. A thing that is ruined is a ___wreck___.

5. To hide a gift in paper is to ___wrap___ it.

6. When you put a story on paper, you ___write___.

7. Your ___wrist___ holds your hand to your arm.

8. A truck that clears away wrecks is a ___wrecker___.

9. A kind of tool is a ___wrench___.

10. One way to fight is to ___wrestle___.

Find **a word in the box that answers each riddle.**
Print **it on the line.**

wren	wrecker	wriggle	wrong	wrist
wrench	wreath	writer	wristwatch	wrinkle

1. I am a useful tool.
   I can fix things.
   What am I?

   Wrench

2. I am the opposite of **right**.
   I rhyme with **song**.
   What am I?

   wrong

3. I can fly.
   I like to sing.
   What am I?

   Wren

4. I am round and pretty.
   You can hang me up.
   What am I?

   wreath

5. I am next to a hand.
   I can twist and bend.
   What am I?

   wrist

6. I tell time.
   People wear me on their wrist.
   What am I?

   wristwatch

7. I am a big truck.
   I tow things away.
   What am I?

   Wrecker

8. I write stories. They can be
   real or make-believe.
   What am I?

   writer

9. I am a fold in a dress.
   I am a crease in a face.
   What am I?

   wrinkle

10. I am another word for **squirm**.
    I rhyme with **giggle**.
    What am I?

    Wriggle

 Ask your child to write sentences
for two of the words on this page.

126   Consonant digraph wr

Name _____

▶ Complete **each sentence with one of the words in the box. Write** the word on the line.

~~your~~	two	~~believe~~
~~once~~	~~bought~~	~~new~~

1. Many people _____believe_____ that animals have feelings.

2. When _____your_____ dog is happy, it will wag its tail.

3. Dolphins seem to enjoy learning _____new_____ tricks.

4. Many pet birds are _____bought_____ and sold in pairs.

5. Having _____two_____ parakeets will keep them from being lonely.

6. A gorilla _____once_____ cared lovingly for a kitten.

7. How do _____your_____ pets show their feelings?

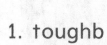 Unscramble **the letters to** write **the words. The word shapes will help you print the words.**

1. toughb  bought

2. eonc 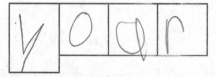 once

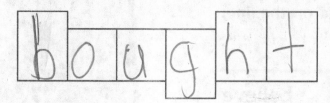

3. ryou  your

4. owt two

5. veliebe  believe

6. ewn new

 CHECKING Put a ✔ next to each word you can read.

 bought   once   your two 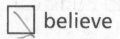 believe   new

 HOME Give your child a magazine and have him or her circle the words taught in this lesson.

Name_____

Phonics & Reading

Read **the story.** Use **a word from the story to finish each sentence.** Print **the word on the line.**

Chipmunks

Chipmunks have brown fur with black-and-white stripes. These colors help the chipmunk blend in with trees and bushes. You might not even see or hear them unless they move, and they can move fast.

The chipmunk is known to build its den or home under rocks or bushes. This is where it stores nuts and seeds. This food will keep the chipmunk from going hungry during the winter.

Chipmunks are fun to watch. You may have seen one wriggle its nose as it turns a nut over and over with its paws. Chipmunks carry nuts and other food in their cheek pouches. A chipmunk with bulging cheeks is really cute!

1. This story is about ___chipmunks___.

2. Chipmunks build their dens under rocks or ___bushes___.

3. Their fur has black-and- ___white___ stripes.

4. The chipmunk can ___wriggle___ its nose.

Why might a chipmunk be fun to watch?

Use **a digraph tile to finish each of the words below.** Write **the digraphs on the lines.**

| wh | ck | ch | kn |

1. _ch_ irp
2. _Wh_ ale
3. _kn_ ot

| th | sh | wr | ck |

4. flo _ck_
5. tee _th_
6. swi _sh_

| wr | th | ch | kn |

7. _kn_ ees
8. _wrn_ ench
9. _th_ umb

| ck | sh | wh | ch |

10. bun _ch_
11. clo _ck_
12. fi _sh_

▶ Write **sentences for two of the words you made.**

The wholes teeth
are so big.

Work with your child to make a word ladder beginning or ending with any of the words he or she made.

Name_____

So many strawberries to pick,
It's hard to know where to start!
Let's pick the largest ones
And bake them in a tart:

RULE

An **r** after a vowel makes the vowel sound different from the usual short or long sound. You can hear the **ar** sound in **hard**, **start**, and **largest.**

▶ Find **the word in the box that will finish each sentence. Print it on the line.**

apart	star	hard	part	car
hardly	start	large	jars	

1. I picked out a new model _____ kit.

2. I got two _____ jars _____ of paint, too.

3. I could hardly wait to _____ hardly _____ on it.

4. I used glue so the car wouldn't fall _____ large _____.

5. There were small parts and _____ cars _____ parts.

6. The tires were _____ hard _____ to fit, but I did it.

7. I stuck _____ apart _____ stickers on the sides.

8. I could _____ start _____ believe it when it was done.

9. The best _____ star _____ was showing it to my friends.

Copyright © Savvas Learning Company LLC. All Rights Reserved.

Finish **each sentence**. Use **a word that** rhymes **with the word beside the sentence**. Print **it on the line**.

1. A shark is a very _____smart_____ animal.

2. It lives in the deep, _____dark_____ part of the ocean.

3. It can grow to be very _____large_____.

4. A shark's teeth are very _____sharp_____.

5. It has no problem tearing food _____apart_____.

6. I live _____far_____ from the ocean.

7. I like to visit the animal _____park_____.

8. It is not far from my house by _____car_____.

9. I can watch the sharks there free from _____harm_____.

part

bark

barge

carp

start

car

lark

tar

farm

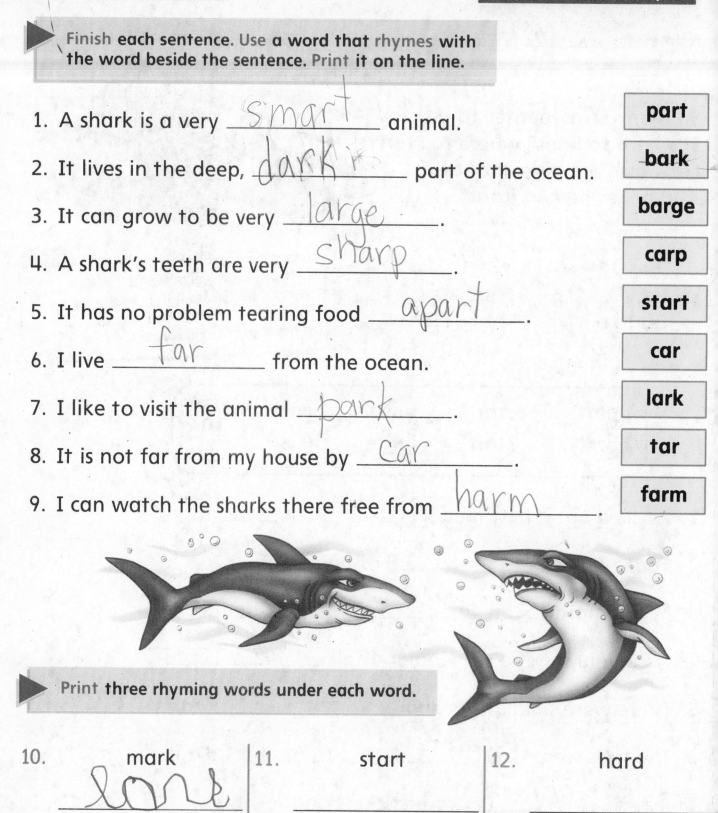

Print **three rhyming words under each word**.

10.   mark
_____lark_____

_____

_____

11.   start
_____

_____

_____

12.   hard
_____

_____

_____

HOME

Ask your child to list words that rhyme with *car*.

Name _____

Corn is such a tasty treat
In any form you please.
It is much more fun to eat
Than broccoli or peas.

Copyright © Savvas Learning Company LLC. All Rights Reserved.

► Read **each riddle. Answer it with a word that** rhymes **with the word beside the riddle. Print it on the line.**

RULE

An **r** after a vowel makes the vowel sound different from the usual short or long sound. You can hear the **or** sound in **corn** and **more**.

1. Something we can pop and eat _____

2. Something on a unicorn _____

3. Something we eat with _____

4. Something with rain, wind, and thunder _____

5. Something we can play or watch _____

6. Something sharp on a rose _____

7. Something beside the sea _____

8. Something to close up a bottle _____

9. Something that gives us light _____

| horn |
| born |
| cork |
| form |
| port |
| born |
| tore |
| pork |
| porch |

Help **the horse get to the barn. Find the words in the maze with ar and or.** Follow **them to get to the barn. Write each word on the line beside the puzzle.**

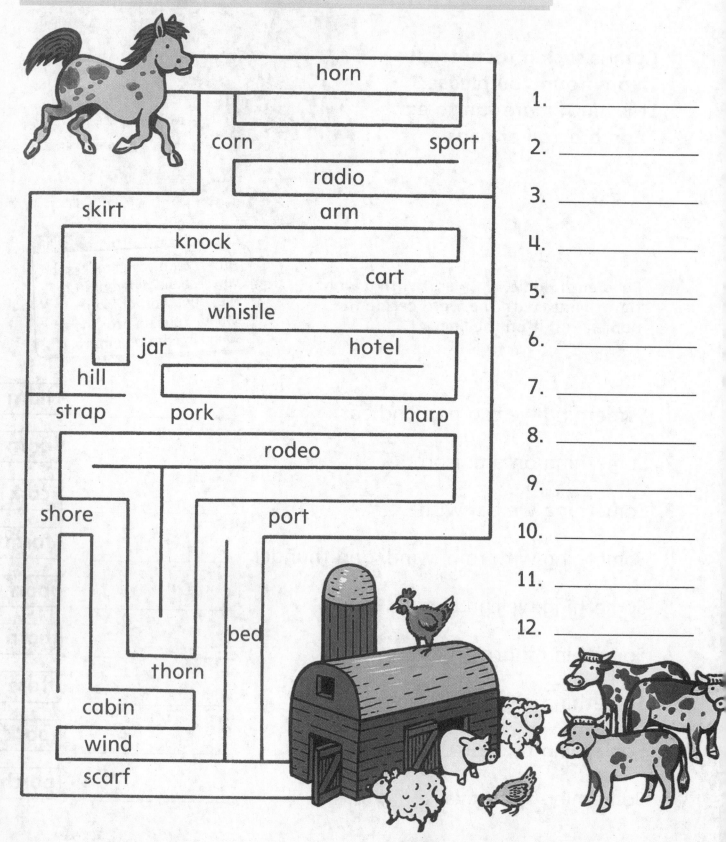

horn

corn   sport

radio

skirt   arm

knock

cart

whistle

jar   hotel

hill

strap   pork   harp

rodeo

shore   port

bed

thorn

cabin

wind

scarf

1. _____

2. _____

3. _____

4. _____

5. _____

6. _____

7. _____

8. _____

9. _____

10. _____

11. _____

12. _____

134 Review words with ar, or

HOME Have your child separate the words in the list into two groups: *ar* words and *or* words.

Name _____

See that bird in the old fir tree?
She'll turn around and chirp at me.
She chirps and chirps her song all day.
I hope she never ever goes away.

▶ Circle **each word that has the same vowel sound as the name of the picture.**

RULE

An **r** after a vowel makes the vowel sound different from the usual short or long sound. You can hear the **ir** sound in **bird**, the **ur** sound in **turn**, and the **er** sound in **her**.

1. **ir**

bird

first
fork
skirt
shirt
girl

2. **ur**

turtle

curb
purse
card
nurse
fur

3. **er**

fern

batter
letter
hammer
park
clerk

▶ Find **the name of each picture in the words above.** Print **the name on the line.**

4.

_____

5.

_____

6.

_____

7.

_____

8.

_____

9.

_____

10.

_____

11.

_____

Copyright © Savvas Learning Company LLC. All Rights Reserved.

Words with ir, er, ur: Picture-text match   **135**

Underline **the name of the picture.** Circle **the box that has the same vowel with r.**

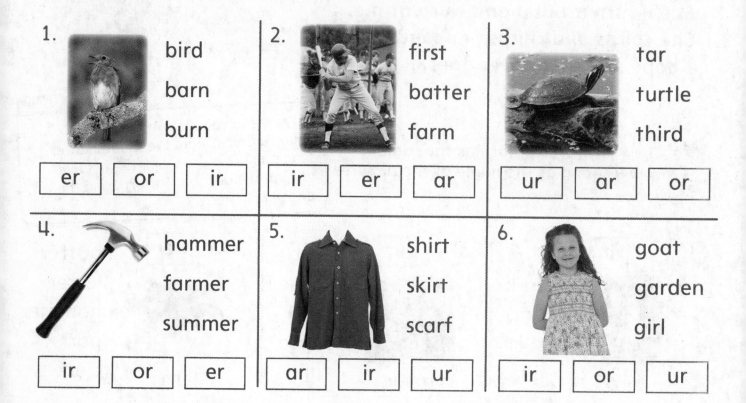

1.
bird
barn
burn

| er | or | ir |

2.
first
batter
farm

| ir | er | ar |

3.
tar
turtle
third

| ur | ar | or |

4.
hammer
farmer
summer

| ir | or | er |

5.
shirt
skirt
scarf

| ar | ir | ur |

6.
goat
garden
girl

| ir | or | ur |

Circle **the word that will finish the sentence.** Print **it on the line.**

7. Dogs have _____ and bark.   far   fur

8. Birds have feathers and _____.   cheat   chirp

9. Kittens _____ up when they nap.   curl   car

10. Fish have fins and swim in the _____.   river   hurt

11. Worms wiggle and live in _____.   burn   dirt

12. Have you _____ wondered why?   other   ever

136   Words with ir, er, ur: Words in context

HOME

Help your child list the words on
the page that contain *ir, er,* or *ur.*

Name_____

Say and spell each word in the box below. Then, print the word on the line where it belongs.

shoe	beach	truck	wheel	car	girl
write	thorn	why	chair	wrong	nurse
knit	fork	knock	wish	bath	block

sh

1. _____

2. _____

th

3. _____

4. _____

wh

5. _____

6. _____

ch

7. _____

8. _____

ck

9. _____

10. _____

kn

11. _____

12. _____

ir, ur

13. _____

14. _____

wr

15. _____

16. _____

ar, or

17. _____

18. _____

Copyright © Savvas Learning Company LLC. All Rights Reserved.

Phonics & Writing

A **news story** tells a story about an event that just happened. It should tell *who* or *what* the event is about, *when* and *where* it happened, and *why* or *how* it happened. The *headline* gives the reader clues about the event.

Pretend someone you know just won a prize for growing the largest pumpkin in town. **Write** a news story about it. **Use** some of the words in the box.

dirt	water	when	each	know
this	brother	write	where	little
show	start	rocks	large	yard

Begin with a headline.

_____

_____

_____

_____

Tell *who* or *what* the story is about.

_____

_____

_____

_____

Tell *when*, *where*, *why,* or *how* it happened.

_____

_____

_____

138 Words with sh, th, wh, ch, ck, kn, wr; r-controlled vowels

HOME Ask your child to circle the words in the news story he or she wrote, with digraphs and r-controlled vowels.

Name

The Gray Wolf

Gray wolves are known to be among the smartest animals. They live in packs or families. They are loyal to members of their own pack. They eat and play together. They even all help care for their young.

 1

FOLD

Copyright © Savvas Learning Company LLC. All Rights Reserved.

The gray wolf is *endangered*. This means that very few of them are alive. Soon, there might be no more gray wolves anywhere. We can save the gray wolf by choosing to share the earth with wild animals.

4

The howl of the gray wolf can be heard at any time of day or night. Wolves howl to call the pack together before or after a hunt. They howl to find one another, or to warn other packs to stay away.

2

Wolves are meat eaters. They hunt either alone or with the pack. When an animal is caught, the pack eats its fill. Then, animals such as the fox or coyote, get the leftovers so there is no waste.

3

Name _____

Copyright © Savvas Learning Company LLC. All Rights Reserved.

▶ **Fill in the bubble beside the name of each picture.**

1.
○ nice
○ mice
○ rice

2.
○ giraffe
○ goat
○ giant

3.
○ turn
○ train
○ turkey

4.
○ popcorn
○ cupcake
○ pencil

5.
○ beach
○ dirt
○ bird

6.
○ clock
○ cherry
○ check

7.
○ block
○ black
○ blot

8.
○ sneak
○ snake
○ snore

9.
○ skunk
○ skate
○ skill

10.
○ bun
○ bunny
○ baby

11.
○ try
○ cry
○ shy

12.
○ ship
○ shop
○ shell

13.
○ trunk
○ think
○ thirteen

14.
○ chair
○ table
○ turtle

15.
○ wrap
○ write
○ wriggle

Compounds; le; hard and soft c, g; blends; vowel y; digraphs; r-controlled vowels: Assessment

141

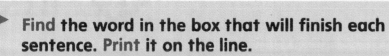

Find **the word in the box that will finish each sentence. Print it on the line.**

knife	garden	Maybe
peppers	who	corn
celery	fresh	glad

1. Many kinds of vegetables grow in a _____.

2. The _____ is green and leafy.

3. We need a _____ to cut the stalks.

4. Both red and green _____ taste good in a salad.

5. _____ I can eat one of the peppers right now.

6. Let's go pick some sweet yellow _____.

7. Vegetables taste best when they are _____.

8. I'm _____ it's almost time to eat.

9. Now _____ will cook them for us?

Can you read each word? **Put a ✔ in the box if you can.**

☐ only   ☐ own   ☐ their   ☐ laugh   ☐ even   ☐ might

☐ your   ☐ two   ☐ believe   ☐ once   ☐ bought   ☐ new

HOME

Ask your child to make up new sentences containing some of the words from the box.

Read Aloud

Traveling in Space

You may wonder what the crew of the shuttle does in space. Sometimes the space crew works to find out more about our own planet. Looking at Earth from space helps the crew see things we can't see from the ground.

Photos taken from space can tell us about earthquakes, volcanoes, and storms. They can even help people on the ground find forest fires.

TALK About It

In what other ways might space travel help us learn about Earth?

Dear Family,

In this unit about space, your child will be learning about contractions, word endings, and suffixes. As your child becomes familiar with these forms, you might like to try these activities together.

▶ Read the selection on page 143 with your child. Talk about space travel with him or her. Together, identify contractions, such as you've and can't, words with endings, such as zooms and looking, and words with suffixes, such as higher and loudest.

▶ With your child, look through newspapers and magazines for articles about space. Read the articles and circle words with contractions, endings, and suffixes.

You and your child might enjoy reading these books together.

Sun, Moon, and Stars
by Mary Hoffman and Jane Ray

Space Busters by Philip Wilkinson

Sincerely,

_____

Destination: Mars

Traveling to Mars isn't a new idea. We've done it for 25 years using robotic rovers. What is new is getting humans to land on Mars. Mars is farther than anywhere humans have traveled in space to date. The current Space Shuttle isn't built to travel this far. NASA is working on new ways to get us to Mars.

Estimada familia:

En esta unidad, que trata sobre el espacio, su hijo/a aprenderá contracciones, terminaciones de palabras y sufijos. A medida que su hijo/a se vaya familiarizando con estas formas, pueden hacer las siguientes actividades juntos.

▶ Lean con su hijo/a la selección en la página 143. Hablen sobre los viajes espaciales. Juntos, identifiquen contracciones, como por ejemplo you've y can't, terminaciones de palabras como zooms y looking, y palabras con sufijos, como higher y loudest.

▶ Busquen con su hijo/a artículos sobre el espacio en revistas y periódicos. Lean los artículos y encierren en un círculo las palabras con contracciones, las terminaciones y los sufijos.

Ustedes y su hijo/a disfrutarán leyendo estos libros juntos.

Sun, Moon, and Stars
de Mary Hoffman y Jane Ray

Space Busters de Philip Wilkinson

Sinceramente,

_____

Copyright © Savvas Learning Company LLC. All Rights Reserved.

Name_____

I'll build a rocket.
We'll go to the moon.
We'll explore outer space.
You'll be home by noon.

RULE

A **contraction** is a short way of writing two words. It is formed by putting two words together and leaving out one or more letters. An apostrophe (') is used to show where something is left out. Some contractions are formed with the word **will**.

I will = I'll

▶ Print **a contraction from the box that means the same as the two words beside each line.**

you'll	they'll	she'll
we'll	I'll	he'll

1. I will _____ 2. he will _____

3. we will _____ 4. they will _____

5. she will _____ 6. you will _____

▶ Print **the short form of the two underlined words in each sentence.**

7. <u>I will</u> get in the boat after you. _____

8. <u>He will</u> climb aboard next. _____

9. <u>She will</u> join us, too. _____

10. <u>They will</u> hop in for the ride. _____

11. All aboard? Oh, no! <u>We will</u> sink! _____

Copyright © Savvas Learning Company LLC. All Rights Reserved.

Print a contraction from the box that means the same as the two words beside each line.

RULE
Some contractions are formed with the word **not**.
does not = doesn't

can't	couldn't	weren't	doesn't	don't
didn't	aren't	isn't	won't	haven't

1. are not _____

2. do not _____

3. did not _____

4. will not _____

5. were not _____

6. is not _____

7. could not _____

8. can not _____

9. does not _____

10. have not _____

Print two words that mean the same as each underlined word.

11. Mitten the kitten <u>can't</u> get down from the tree. _____

12. She <u>isn't</u> brave enough to climb down. _____

13. She <u>doesn't</u> know what to do. _____

14. We <u>didn't</u> have any problem getting her down. _____

15. "<u>Aren't</u> you a lucky kitten to have friends to help?" _____

Contractions with not: Words in context, high-frequency words

 With your child, take turns forming contractions with the words *will* and *not*.

Name _____

Read **the letter. Print a contraction on the line** to finish each sentence.

July 10

Dear Mom and Dad,

I can't believe I've been at Space Camp for four days. I'm having so much fun. I don't ever want to leave!

We're being trained like real astronauts. We made models of rockets. Yesterday, we launched them and mine worked! It's hard work. There's so much to remember.

Today, I'll take my place at Mission Control. There, I will use a computer to help our flight crew lift off using the sights and sounds of a real space mission. I can't wait!

Love

Copyright © Savvas Learning Company LLC. All Rights Reserved.

1. Cara said, "I _____ believe _____ been at Sp_____ ____r four days."

2. "_____ being trained like real astronauts," _____ she said.

3. "_____ hard work. _____ so much to remember."

 How might a computer be used to help astronauts in space?

Review contractions: Critical thinking   **151**

Use **a word tile to make contractions with not, have, will, or is. Write** each contraction on the lines.

| do | are | let | have |

not

1. _don't_

2. _aren't_

3. _havn't_

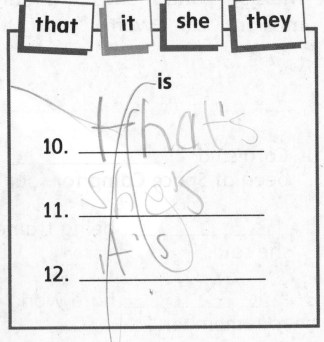

| you | we | she | they |

have

4. _you've_

5. _we've_

6. _they've_

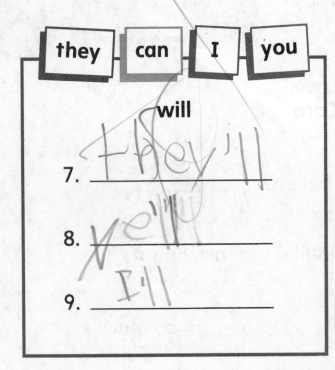

| they | can | I | you |

will

7. _they'll_

8. _we'll_

9. _I'll_

| that | it | she | they |

is

10. _that's_

11. _she's_

12. _it's_

Ask your child to write sentences for the contractions on the page.

Name _____

Sandwiches, books, a snack—
What things shall I pack?
I'll blast off to Mars,
And zoom past the stars!

▶ Circle **the word that will finish each sentence.** Print **it on the line.**

RULE

When **s** or **es** is added to a word it forms the plural. Plural means "more than one." If a word ends in **x, z, ss, sh,** or **ch,** usually add **es** to make it mean more than one. For other words just add **s.**

one brush	two **brushes**
one sandwich	many **sandwiches**
one book	three **books**

1. At the zoo we saw some

   seal   seals

   _____.

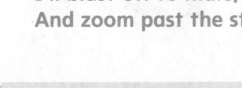

2. We like to eat fresh

   peach   peaches

   _____.

3. We have toys in three

   box   boxes

   _____.

4. June will use a

   brush   brushes

   _____.

5. Ed's mom gave him a

   cap   caps

   _____.

6. Just look at those

   dog   dogs

   _____.

7. Look at those shiny

   star   stars

   _____.

8. The box was used for

   mitten   mittens

   _____.

Copyright © Savvas Learning Company LLC. All Rights Reserved.

Read **each** shopping list. **Finish each** word by adding the ending **s** or **es**. **Print** the ending on the line.

1.

Steve's List

2 book __s__ to read

3 paintbrush __es__

6 red pencil __s__

2 jar __s__ of paste

2.

Peggy's List

5 block __s__

2 box __es__ of clay

3 top __s__ to spin

2 puzzle __s__

3.

Pam's List

8 dish __es__

8 cup __s__

4 glass __es__

2 patch __es__ for jeans

4.

Ron's List

7 apple __s__

5 peach __es__

4 sandwich __es__

2 bunch __es__ of grapes

HOME Ask your child to make up a list of objects using endings -s, -es.

Name _____

Floating and bobbing,
We drifted in space.
We tried hard to run,
But just stayed in one place.

> **RULE**
>
> A **base word** is a word to which the ending **ing** or **ed** can be added to form a new word.
>
> float + ing = floating
> drift + ed = drifted

▶ Add **ing** to each base word.
Print **the new word on the line.**

1. sleep _____   2. jump _____

3. play _____   4. help _____

5. start _____   6. work _____

7. fish _____   8. turn _____

▶ Add **ing** to the word beside each sentence. Print **the new word on the line.**

9. We are _____ for the bus.

10. Doris and Mark are _____ rope.

11. Sam is _____ for the bus.

12. Bart's dog is _____ with him.

13. Terry is _____ his lunch.

14. Meg is _____ a book.

15. Now, the bus is _____ our corner!

| wait |
| jump |
| look |
| stay |
| hold |
| read |
| turn |

Copyright © Savvas Learning Company LLC. All Rights Reserved.

Add **ed** to each base word. Print the new word on the line. Use the new words to finish the sentences.

1. look

_____

2. want

_____

3. help

_____

4. leap

_____

5. fix

_____

6. paint

_____

7. Jess _____ me catch a frog.

8. We _____ a frog for a pet.

9. We _____ everywhere for frogs.

10. Suddenly, a frog _____ over a rock.

11. We _____ up a box as a frog home.

Print **each base word on the line.**

12. locked

_____

13. marched

_____

14. dreamed

_____

15. played

_____

16. cleaned

_____

17. passed

_____

18. watched

_____

19. wanted

_____

20. missed

_____

HOME With your child, take turns acting out each base word; then add -ed.

Name _____

Copyright © Savvas Learning Company LLC. All Rights Reserved.

▶ Add **ing** to the base word in the box.
Print **the new word on the line.**

RULE

When a short vowel word ends in a single consonant, usually double the consonant before adding **ing.**
stop + ing = stopping

1. Maria and Dana were _____ to go shopping.

| plan |

2. First, they went _____ in the park.

| walk |

3. Children were _____ on the swings.

| swing |

4. A cat was _____ in the shade.

| nap |

5. People were _____ along a path.

| jog |

6. Dana saw two bunnies _____ by.

| hop |

7. Maria's ice cream cone was _____.

| drip |

8. They saw a man _____ hot dogs.

| roast |

9. His dog was _____ for one.

| beg |

10. "_____ by the park was fun," said Maria.

| Stop |

11. "Now, let's go _____," Dana said.

| shop |

 TALK About It

What time of year is this?

Inflectional ending -ing: High-frequency words, critical thinking   **157**

Add **ed** to the word beside each sentence to make it tell about the past. Print **the word on the line.**

RULE

To make a word tell about the past, usually add **ed.** If a short vowel word ends in a single consonant, usually double the consonant before adding **ed.** I **skip** on my way home. Yesterday I **skipped,** too.

1. My dog _____ his tail when I got home.

2. He _____ up on me with a happy smile.

3. I _____ back because he was muddy.

4. "Wags, you need to be _____!"

5. I _____ him up and put him in the tub.

6. I _____ him with soap and rinsed him.

7. He _____ water everywhere!

8. Then, he _____ all over my floor.

9. I laughed as I _____ him.

10. When Wags _____, he was clean but the bathroom was a mess!

11. I _____ up the mess.

12. Then, I _____ with Wags.

wag

jump

step

scrub

pick

rub

splash

drip

watch

stop

mop

play

TALK About It

How do you think Wags got muddy?

Inflectional ending -ed: High-frequency words, critical thinking

HOME

Take turns with your child saying and spelling a word with the -ed ending.

Name _____

Copyright © Savvas Learning Company LLC. All Rights Reserved.

▶ Circle **the word that finishes each sentence.** Print **it on the line.**

> **RULE**
> If a word ends with a silent **e**, drop the **e** before adding **ing** or **ed**.
> I **bake** cookies with my mom.
> We **baked** cookies yesterday.
> We are **baking** cookies today, too.

1. Yesterday, I _____ to the park.

jogged
jogging

2. Then, I _____ home.

walked
walking

3. Today, I am _____ with friends.

skating
skated

4. We are _____ for lunch.

stopped
stopping

▶ Read **each pair of sentences.** Add **ing** or **ed** to the base word. Print **the new word on the line.**

clean

5. Today, Dad is _____ the garage.

He _____ the car yesterday.

save

6. I am _____ my money to buy a bike.

Last week, I _____ about $3.00.

wag

7. Last night, my dog was happy, so she _____ her tail. She is _____ her tail now, too.

▶ Add **ing** to each base word. Print **the new word on the line.**

1. ride _____

2. fry _____

3. rub _____

4. hide _____

5. frame _____

6. dig _____

7. take _____

8. jump _____

9. poke _____

10. ship _____

11. pack _____

12. quit _____

▶ Add **ed** to each base word. Print **the new word on the line.**

13. pin _____

14. rock _____

15. chase _____

16. hop _____

17. march _____

18. bake _____

19. wish _____

20. drop _____

21. hope _____

22. quack _____

160 Inflectional endings -ing, -ed: Spelling

With your child, take turns choosing a word, adding an ending, and then using the new word in a sentence.

Name _____

Read the story. **Print** a word that ends in **s, es, ed,** or **ing** on the line to finish each sentence.

The Sun:
Star of Our Solar System

The sun shines on us giving Earth light and heat. Without the sun, Earth would be so cold that no plants and animals would be able to live there. That is why the sun is so important.

The sun is a star. Like other stars, the sun is made of burning gases. From Earth, the sun looks like a glowing yellow ball because of the burning gases. The sun is closer to us than other stars, so it seems larger. Earth and the other planets move around the sun. The sun and the planets are called the solar system.

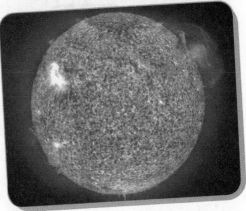

1. The sun shines on us, _____ Earth light and heat.

2. Like other stars, the sun is made up of burning _____.

3. The sun is closer to us than other _____ , so it seems larger.

4. The sun and the planets are _____ the solar system.

 Would there be life on Earth without the sun? Why or why not?

Review -s, -es, -ed, -ing: Critical thinking   **161**

Copyright © Savvas Learning Company LLC. All Rights Reserved.

Phonics & Writing

Add the ending to each word inside the box. You may have to change the spelling of a word before adding the ending.

s or es

1. star _____
2. dish _____
3. moon _____
4. lunch _____

ing

5. stop _____
6. fly _____
7. walk _____
8. shine _____

ed

9. fix _____
10. step _____
11. play _____
12. save _____

s or es

13. fox _____
14. jump _____
15. buzz _____
16. watch _____

▶ Write a sentence using one or more of the words you made.

_____

_____

_____

162   Review -s, -es, -ed, -ing: Writing

HOME
Ask your child to write sentences for three of the other words on the page.

Name _____

A handful of moon dust,
A lunar rock or two—
Visiting the moon must
Be wonderful to do!

Copyright © Savvas Learning Company LLC. All Rights Reserved.

► Add **the ending ful to each base word.** Print **the new word on the line. Use the new words** to finish the sentences.

RULE
You can make a new word by adding the ending **ful** to a base word.
color + ful = colorful

1. care _____

2. cheer _____

3. wonder _____

4. hope _____

5. Pablo was _____ that he could have a new scooter.

6. He promised to be _____ if he got one.

7. His family looked _____ when they gave him his gift.

8. It was a scooter! What a _____ gift!

► Draw **a box around each base word.**

9. u s e f u l

10. h o p e f u l

11. r e s t f u l

12. h a r m f u l

13. f e a r f u l

14. h e l p f u l

15. p l a y f u l

16. c a r e f u l

Suffix -ful: Words in context   **163**

What's that in the darkness?
A space monster in flight?
I'm almost fearless,
But I'll turn on the light!

RULE

You can add the ending
ness or **less** to a base word
to make a new word.
dark + ness = darkness
fear + less = fearless

▶ Add **less** or **ness** to each base word.
Print **the new word on the line. Use
the new words to finish the sentences.**

less	ness

1. use _____   5. weak _____

2. sleep _____   6. dark _____

3. harm _____   7. loud _____

4. fear _____   8. sharp _____

9. It is _____ to tell me bears are harmless.

10. I am not brave or _____ .

11. If I think about bears when I'm in bed, I'm _____ .

12. The bear's eyes are glowing in the _____ .

13. The _____ of their snarls worries me.

14. I can almost feel the _____ of their teeth.

15. I wish that bears were known for _____ .

HOME   Write base words and suffixes on
separate cards and have your child
match them.

Name_____

Slowly, the sun rises.
Quickly, the sky gets bright.
Slowly, the sun will set again,
When it's nearly night.

> **Add the ending ly to each base word.
> Print the new word on the line.**

RULE
Add the ending **ly** to a base word to make a new word.
slow + ly = slowly

1. close _____

2. swift _____

3. soft _____

4. brave _____

5. loud _____

6. slow _____

7. love _____

8. near _____

> **Circle each ly ending in the sentences. Print the base words on the lines.**

9. Tigers walk softly. _____

10. Lions roar bravely. _____

11. Monkeys screech loudly. _____

12. Turtles crawl slowly. _____

13. Deer run swiftly. _____

14. I watch the animals closely at the zoo. _____

15. The zoo near my house is lovely. _____

Copyright © Savvas Learning Company LLC. All Rights Reserved.

Match the base word in the first column with the new word in the second column. Print the letter on the line.

1.

_____ quick   a. slowly

_____ sweet   b. quickly

_____ slow   c. sweetly

_____ loud   d. loudly

_____ nice   e. nicely

2.

_____ glad   a. softly

_____ soft   b. nearly

_____ near   c. lovely

_____ love   d. gladly

_____ brave   e. bravely

3.

_____ use   a. playful

_____ play   b. handful

_____ cheer   c. useful

_____ hand   d. harmful

_____ harm   e. cheerful

4.

_____ care   a. fearless

_____ sleeve   b. helpless

_____ fear   c. endless

_____ end   d. careless

_____ help   e. sleeveless

5.

_____ home   a. sleepless

_____ sleep   b. hopeless

_____ use   c. homeless

_____ wire   d. useless

_____ hope   e. wireless

6.

_____ good   a. softness

_____ dark   b. sadness

_____ kind   c. darkness

_____ sad   d. goodness

_____ soft   e. kindness

HOME With your child, think of other word pairs to add to the boxes.

Name _____

Earth is nearer to our sun
Than planets such as Mars.
But Mercury is the nearest one
To the sun, our nearest star.

▶ **Add the ending er and est to each word. Print the new words on the lines.**

You can add the ending **er** to a base word to make a new word that tells about two things. Add the ending **est** to tell about more than two things.
bright brighter brightest

er	est

1. near _____ _____

2. long _____ _____

3. fast _____ _____

4. dark _____ _____

5. thick _____ _____

6. deep _____ _____

7. soft _____ _____

▶ **Draw a picture to show the meaning of each word.**

8.	9.	10.
long	longer	longest

Copyright © Savvas Learning Company LLC. All Rights Reserved.

Finish **each sentence by adding er or est to each base word. Use er to tell about two things. Use est to tell about more than two things. Print the new word on the line.**

1. tall   Meg is ———————— than Jay.

2. hard   The rock is ———————— than the soap.

3. fast   The horse is the ———————— of the three.

4. long   The top fish is the ————————.

5. cold   Ice is ———————— than water.

6. small   The ant is the ————————.

With your child, take turns using -er and -est words to compare things at home.

Name _____

RULE

► Add **er** and **est** to each word.
Print **the new words on the lines.**

When a word ends in **y** after a
consonant, change the **y** to **i** before
adding **er** or **est.**
busy + est = busiest

er	est
1. silly _____	_____
2. happy _____	_____
3. windy _____	_____
4. fluffy _____	_____

► Finish **each sentence by adding er or est to the base**
word beside each sentence. Print **it on the line.**

5. Today was Justin's _____ day of
the week.

happy

6. He got to the bus stop _____ than
he had on the other days.

early

7. It was _____ than it had been
all week.

sunny

8. He made up the _____ joke
he could.

silly

9. The other kids said it was the

funny

_____ one they had heard.

Copyright © Savvas Learning Company LLC. All Rights Reserved.

RULE
When a word ends in **y** after a consonant, change the **y** to **i** before adding **es**.
story + es = stories

▶ **Circle the name of each picture.**

1.

daisy   daisies

2.

cherry   cherries

3.

lily   lilies

▶ **Use the rule to add es to the word beside each sentence. Finish the sentence by printing the new word on the line.**

4. We wrote _____ for our class book.

story

5. Mine was about my dog's new _____.

puppy

6. Lily wrote about planting _____.

daisy

7. Penny's story was about raising _____.

bunny

8. Carol told us about picking _____.

cherry

9. Marty gave ideas for birthday _____.

party

10. Jerry told how to take care of _____.

pony

11. Tony wrote about his collection of _____.

penny

12. When we finished, we made extra _____.

copy

 HOME With your child, take turns choosing a base word, adding -es, and using it in a sentence.

Name _____

 Add **endings to make the words mean more than one.**

1. bunny	2. city	3. box
_____	_____	_____
4. lily	5. dress	6. pony
_____	_____	_____

▶ **Circle the word that will finish each sentence. Print it on the line. Then, print the name of each picture below.**

7. Mary's birthday _____ was fun.   party   parties

8. Her dad read scary _____.   story   stories

9. We tossed _____ into bottles.   penny   pennies

10. Instead of cake, we ate _____ pie.   cherry   cherries

11. We got little _____ to take home.   candy   candies

12.	13.	14.

_____	_____	_____

Copyright © Savvas Learning Company LLC. All Rights Reserved.

Change **the y to i and add es to the word in each box. Print the new word to finish the sentence.**

1. Farms are not found in _____.

city

2. Sometimes my friends and our _____ visit a farm.

family

3. Sometimes there are _____ in the fields.

daisy

4. _____ often grow by the streams.

Lily

5. We like to ride the _____.

pony

6. There are many different animal _____.

baby

7. It's fun to play with the _____.

bunny

8. We usually see some _____.

puppy

9. Apples and _____ grow on farms.

berry

10. We climb trees to pick _____.

cherry

11. I like to write _____ about our trips to the country.

story

12. I give _____ to my friends to read.

copy

 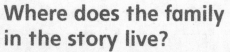 **Where does the family in the story live?**

 Work with your child to write a story using the plural form of some of the words in the boxes above.

Suffix -es for words ending in y: High-frequency words, critical thinking

Name _____

Print **two** words from the list next to the matching ending. For the last one, print **two** contractions.

coldness	going	can't	thoughtful	lovely	funnier
blasted	waiting	darkness	deepest	glasses	bushes
happiest	wanted	slowly	careful	brighter	they're

1. **ed** _____ _____

2. **ing** _____ _____

3. **ly** _____ _____

4. **ful** _____ _____

5. **es** _____ _____

6. **ness** _____ _____

7. **er** _____ _____

8. **est** _____ _____

9. **contractions** _____ _____

Copyright © Savvas Learning Company LLC. All Rights Reserved.

A **log** is a kind of notebook where you write about things you see around you. Keeping a log can help you remember places you visit and things you do each day.

▶ Imagine you were the first astronaut ever to walk on the moon. **Write** about what it was like to walk on the moon. Tell how the moon looked and felt. Some of the words in the box may help you.

lighter	finest	lovelier	bouncing	darkness
it's	hopped	walking	weightless	wished
wonderful	happiest	hopes	I'll	slowly

Write the date to help you remember when you walked on the moon.

Tell about what you saw, heard, and touched.

174   **Contractions, endings, suffixes**

Ask your child to write a sentence for each of the words not included in his or her log entry.

Copyright © Savvas Learning Company LLC. All Rights Reserved.

Name _____

In Space

The spacecraft blasts off. It soars swiftly into the cloudless sky. It climbs higher and higher. As it speeds into the darkness, it moves farther away from our wonderful planet Earth.

1

Life outside the spacecraft is even harsher. Astronauts wear flight suits when they leave the spacecraft and go into space. If they didn't, they wouldn't be able to breathe.

4

In space, everything is weightless. It's not easy to keep your feet on the ground.

Eating your meals in space can be especially tricky. Hold onto your lunch, or it will float away!

2

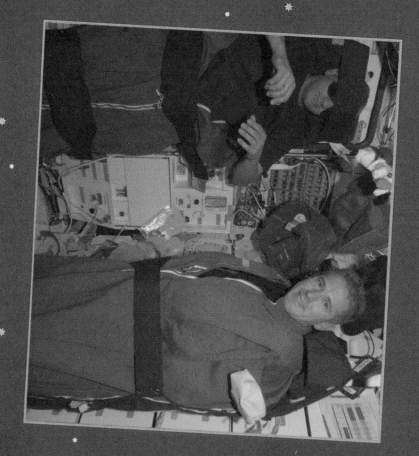

Sleeping in space is strange too. Some astronauts just float in the cabin. Others sleep in beds strapped to the wall.

3

Name _____

> Fill in **the bubble beside the word that names or describes each picture.**

1.
   - ○ box
   - ○ socks
   - ○ boxes

2.
   - ○ fishing
   - ○ sleeping
   - ○ runs

3.
   - ○ glass
   - ○ guess
   - ○ glasses

4.
   - ○ puppy
   - ○ ponies
   - ○ puppies

5.
   - ○ daisy
   - ○ daisies
   - ○ days

6.
   - ○ dish
   - ○ ditches
   - ○ dishes

7. ⭐
   - ○ star
   - ○ stars
   - ○ start

8.
   - ○ peaches
   - ○ peach
   - ○ beach

9.
   - ○ mailing
   - ○ nails
   - ○ sailed

10.
   - ○ baked
   - ○ bank
   - ○ back

11.
   - ○ raking
   - ○ baking
   - ○ jumped

12.
   - ○ racing
   - ○ reading
   - ○ walked

Copyright © Savvas Learning Company LLC. All Rights Reserved.

Contractions, endings, suffixes: Assessment   **177**

▶ **Find the word in the box that will finish each sentence. Print the word on the line.**

strangest	fearful	waited	happily
quietly	biggest	We're	darkness
longer	couldn't	watched	brightest

1. The spaceship arrived _____.

2. We all _____ it land.

3. We _____ see much from where we were standing.

4. Then, a blinding light filled the _____.

5. It was the _____ light we had ever seen.

6. We _____ in silence as a figure appeared.

7. He was the _____ looking little creature.

8. His ears were long, much _____ than mine.

9. His eyes were huge, the _____ I have seen!

10. We were _____ of what he might do.

11. "_____ looking for pizza," he said.

12. We _____ gave them all the pizza we could find.

HOME

Have your child read the story on this page aloud. Then, ask him or her to give the story a title.

Read Aloud

Something Big Has Been Here

by Jack Prelutsky

Something big has been here,
what it was, I do not know,
for I did not see it coming,
and I did not see it go,
but I hope I never meet it,
if I do, I'm in a fix,
for it left behind its footprints,
they are size nine-fifty-six.

TALK
About it

**Why do you think people
search for dinosaur bones?**

Dear Family,

In this unit about dinosaurs, your child will learn about vowel pairs, vowel digraphs, and diphthongs. As your child becomes familiar with these forms, you might try these activities together.

▶ Reread the poem "Something Big Has Been Here" on page 179 with your child. Talk about the size of the dinosaur. Discuss what people can learn from examining a footprint or a bone of a dinosaur.

▶ Make a clay model of a dinosaur. Help your child to identify and record its parts. Circle words with vowel pairs, such as tail, teeth, and toes; vowel digraphs such as jaw, foot, and head; and diphthongs such as mouth.

Your child might enjoy reading these books with you. Look for them in your local library.

Eyewitness Readers: Dinosaur Dinners by Lee Davis

Asteroid Impact by Douglas Henderson

Sincerely,

head

tail—

Estimada familia:

En esta unidad, que trata sobre dinosaurios, su hijo/a aprenderá las parejas de vocales, digramas de vocales y diptongos. A medida que su hijo/a se vaya familiarizando con estas formas, pueden hacer las siguientes actividades juntos.

▶ Lean de nuevo con su hijo/a el poema "Something Big Has Been Here" ("Algo grande estuvo aquí") en la página 179. Hablen sobre el tamaño del dinosaurio. Conversen sobre lo que se puede aprender a partir del examen de una huella o de un hueso de dinosaurio.

▶ Hagan un modelo de arcilla de un dinosaurio. Ayuden a su hijo/a a identificar y anotar sus partes. Encierren en un círculo las palabras con parejas de vocales, como tail (cola), teeth (dientes) y toes (pezuñas); digramas de vocales como jaw (mandíbula), foot (pata) y head (cabeza); y diptongos como mouth (boca).

▶ Ustedes y su hijo/a disfrutarán leyendo estos libros juntos. Búsquenlos en su biblioteca local.

Eyewitness Readers: Dinosaur Dinners de Lee Davis

Asteroid Impact de Douglas Henderson

Sinceramente,

Copyright © Savvas Learning Company LLC. All Rights Reserved.

Name_____

Dinosaurs once claimed the land,
And then they died away.
Why, we don't quite understand,
But hope to learn some day.

RULE

In a **vowel pair,** two vowels come together to make one long vowel sound. The first vowel stands for the long sound and the second vowel is silent. You can hear the long **a** sound in **claimed** and **day.**

▶ Find **the word in the box that names each picture. Print it on the line.**

sail	pay	rain	tail	hay
tray	spray	chain	nail	

1.

_____

2.

_____

3.

_____

4.

_____

5.

_____

6.

_____

7.

_____

8.

_____

9.

_____

Copyright © Savvas Learning Company LLC. All Rights Reserved.

Find the word in the box that answers each riddle. Print the word on the line.

chain	stain	mailbox	hay	pail	rain	tray
play	paint	May	train	gray	sail	day

1. I ride on railroad tracks. _____

2. You put letters in me. _____

3. I am a blend of black and white. _____

4. If I start, you put on a raincoat. _____

5. I am the month after April. _____

6. I am made of many links. _____

7. I am part of a boat. _____

8. I am an ink spot on a shirt. _____

9. I am piled in a stack. _____

10. I am the opposite of work. _____

11. You can carry water in me. _____

12. I am spread on a wall. _____

13. You carry food on me. _____

14. I come before night. _____

HOME With your child, take turns using a word from the box in a sentence.

Name_____

RULE
Vowel pairs **ee** and **ea** can make the long **e** sound. You can hear the long **e** sound in **jeep** and **seal**.

▶ **Circle the name of each picture.**

1.

sell

seal

seed

2.

bean

bed

bee

3.

jeep

jeans

peep

4.

leaf

lean

leak

5.

jeeps

jeans

jets

6.
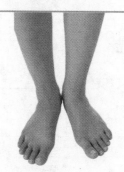

feed

feet

feel

7.

seed

shed

sheep

8.

meat

met

team

9.

beat

beach

beads

10.

peach

peace

pear

11.

seal

seed

send

12.
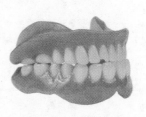

team

test

teeth

Copyright © Savvas Learning Company LLC. All Rights Reserved.

Find the word that will finish each sentence. Print it on the line. Circle the vowel pair in each word.

keep	eager	easy	meal
feet	streams	beaver	tree
teeth	leaves	seem	seen

1. Have you ever _____ a beaver?

2. Beavers live in rivers and _____ .

3. A _____ chews down trees.

4. It makes a _____ of the bark.

5. It uses _____ branches to build a dam.

6. It _____ only the stump behind.

7. A beaver's _____ have to be strong.

8. Its webbed _____ help it swim along.

9. It's not _____ being a beaver.

10. Beavers always _____ to be working.

11. They _____ working until all their work is done.

12. That's why busy people are often called

    "_____ beavers."

 Why is the beaver so busy?

 Help your child sort the words according to vowel pairs (ea or ee).

Name _____

RULE
The vowel pair **ie** sometimes has the long **i** sound. You can hear the long **i** sound in **tie**. The vowel pair **oe** has the long **o** sound. You can hear the long **o** sound in **toe**.

► Circle **the word that will finish each** sentence. Print **it on the line.**

1.

My friend, _____, and I went to the store.

jay
Joe
jot

2.

Along the way, we saw a

_____ by the road.

die
doe
day

3.

When we got there, Joe stubbed his

_____.

tie
toe
lie

4.

My dog _____ stayed outside.

Moe
my
mine

5.

I wanted to buy a new red

_____.

tie
toe
lie

6.

We all had some _____ when we got home.

pie
pine
pile

 Why did Joe and his friend go to the store?

Vowel pairs ie, oe: High-frequency words, critical thinking   **185**

Print **the name for each picture on the line below it.**

RULE
The vowel pair **oe** sometimes has the long **o** sound. The vowel pair **oa** has the long **o** sound. You can hear the long **o** sound in **doe** and **boat**.

| boat | doe | goat | toe | soap | coat |

1. _____

2. _____

3. _____

4. _____

5. _____

6. _____

Circle **the word that will finish each sentence. Print it on the line.**

7. Isn't it fun to ride in a _____?   boot   boat

8. Our friend, _____, has a sailboat.   Joe   joke

9. We _____ across the bay in it.   floated   floor

10. A passing boat splashed water and

_____ us.   soaked   soap

11. I wiggled my _____ in the water.   tone   toes

186   Vowel pairs oa, oe: Words in context

HOME
Have your child make up a story using as many oa and oe words as he or she can.

Name _____

 **Read** the story. **Print** a word with a vowel pair on the line to finish each sentence.

Ray's Surprise

One day, Ray's mom gave him an iguana. It looked like a baby dinosaur. It had a brown and green coat and a long tail. It had big feet with a sharp little claw on each toe.

Ray got a book about iguanas to read. He learned that iguanas don't eat meat. They need a meal of lettuce once a day. They also like sweet potatoes, apples, and oranges. Iguanas need to stay warm and like to lie in the sun. They can grow to be six feet long!

1. Ray's iguana had a long _____ and big _____.

2. Iguanas need a _____ of lettuce once a _____.

3. They also like _____ potatoes.

 Would an iguana make a good pet? Why or why not?

Copyright © Savvas Learning Company LLC. All Rights Reserved.

Phonics & Writing

Use **words with vowel pairs to finish each word ladder.** Change **only one letter at a time.**

1. Begin with **beam**.
   End with **coat**.

   beam

   beat

   boat

   coat

2. Begin with **lean**.
   End with **road**.

   _____

   _____

   _____

   _____

3. Begin with **fried**.
   End with **trees**.

   _____

   _____

   _____

   _____

4. Begin with **dies**.
   End with **goes**.

   _____

   _____

   _____

   _____

HOME With your child, make a word ladder of four words, beginning or ending with any word you made.

Digging for Dinosaurs

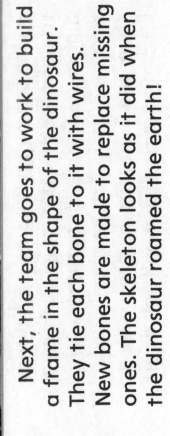

No one has ever seen a dinosaur, so how can we say they ever lived? As layers of rock wore away, people found huge footprints, bones, and teeth called *fossils*. People asked questions and needed answers.

1

Next, the team goes to work to build a frame in the shape of the dinosaur. They tie each bone to it with wires. New bones are made to replace missing ones. The skeleton looks as it did when the dinosaur roamed the earth!

4

Copyright © Savvas Learning Company LLC. All Rights Reserved.

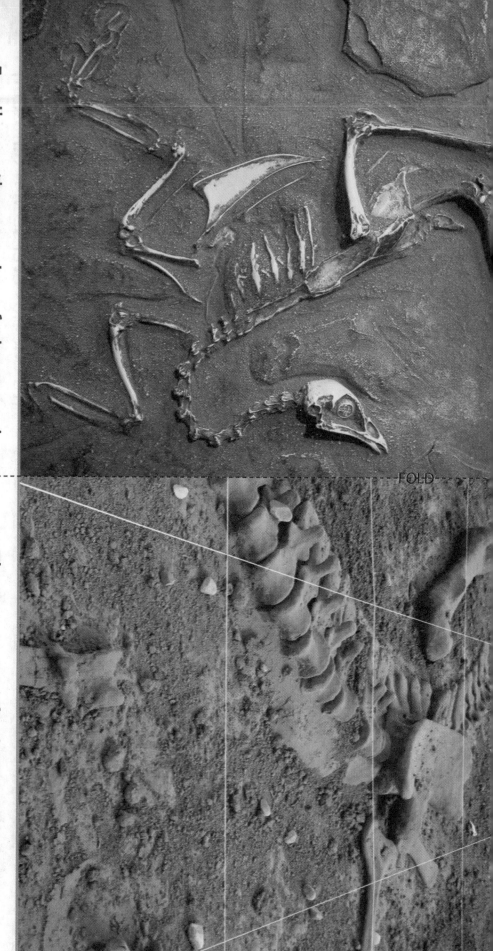

Fossils are the remains of plants and animals that died long ago. Teams of workers find fossils all over the world. It can take days, weeks, or years to find the smallest fossil. It is hard work to find the fossils deep in the rock.

2

The team may find enough bones to put together the main parts of a dinosaur. Pictures of each bone are taken, so there can be no mix-up. Then, the bones are painted with a kind of glue so they won't fall apart.

3

Name _____

We may learn what was not known,
When finding a dinosaur tooth or foot bone.
With tools, scientists chip rocks and look
All around the world, in every nook.

RULE

A vowel digraph is two letters together that stand for one vowel sound. The vowel sound can be long or short, or have a special sound of its own. You can hear the different sounds of the vowel digraph **oo** in **tooth** and **foot**.

▶ **Circle** the word that will finish each sentence. **Print** it on the line.

1. One of my teeth felt a little _____.

   broom
   loose

2. I wanted to see the _____.

   tool
   tooth

3. I ran to my _____.

   room
   zoo

4. I stood on a _____ to look in the mirror.

   spoon
   stool

5. My tooth should fall out _____.

   moon
   soon

6. At _____ it was time for lunch.

   soon
   noon

7. I took a bite of _____ with my spoon.

   food
   fool

8. Out came my loose tooth on the _____.

   soothe
   spoon

9. My friend lost a tooth, _____.

   too
   zoo

What made the loose tooth come out?

Copyright © Savvas Learning Company LLC. All Rights Reserved.

Vowel digraph oo: High-frequency words, critical thinking   **191**

> ► **Find** a word in the box that will finish each sentence. **Print** it on the line.

cookie	look	good	stood
book	cook	took	hook

1. I was looking for a good _____.

2. I took a _____ at a cookbook.

3. I _____ in line to pay for the book.

4. Then, I _____ my new book home.

5. I decided to _____ something.

6. I took my apron off a _____.

7. I tried a _____ recipe.

8. The cookies were very _____.

> ► **Print** the missing letters of each picture's name. **Print** the missing letters for a word that rhymes with it. **Trace** the whole word.

9.

b_____
sh_____

10.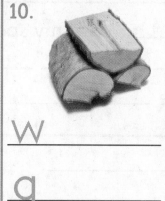

w_____
g_____

11.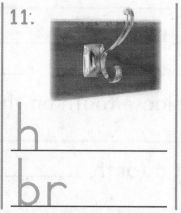

h_____
br_____

12.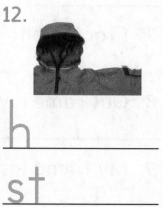

h_____
st_____

192   Vowel digraph oo: Rhyme

With your child, make up a rhyme for each pair of words above.

Name _____

RULE

The vowel digraph **ea** can stand for the short **e** sound. You can hear the short **e** sound in **ready**.

▶ **Find the word in the box that will finish each sentence. Print it on the line.**

ahead	already	breakfast	spread
bread	breath	head	

1. When you wake up, take a deep _____.

2. It will help clear your _____.

3. Now you are ready for _____.

4. Here is some _____ to make toast.

5. You can _____ butter and jam on it.

6. The eggs are _____ made.

7. Go _____ and eat.

▶ **Circle the correct word to finish each sentence.**

8. What is the (feather, weather, leather) like today?

9. Will you need to wear a (sweater, weather, meadow)?

10. Maybe you will need a (ready, heavy, cleanser) coat.

11. Is it cold enough for (bread, thread, leather) boots?

12. Cover your (head, heavy, breakfast) with a warm hat.

13. Now you are (meadow, heavy, ready) to go outside.

Copyright © Savvas Learning Company LLC. All Rights Reserved.

Say the name of each picture. Circle the words with the same ea sound as the picture's name.

1.

bread
weather
seal
leather

2.

bread
beach
heavy
treat

3.

ready
heavy
bread
bean

4.

break
leather
thread
weather

5.

head
heavy
lean
steak

6.

already
meadow
leaves
spread

Circle the word that will finish each sentence. Print it on the line.

7. I have _____ many books about dinosaurs.

ready   read

8. Dinosaurs were _____ before people lived.

dead   head

9. I _____ knew some dinosaurs ate only plants.

already   steady

10. Many dinosaurs were very _____.

heavy   ahead

HOME

With your child, take turns naming words that rhyme with some of the words he or she circled.

Name _____

> Find **the word in the box that will finish each sentence. Print it on the line.**

RULE

The vowel digraphs **au** and **aw** usually have the same sound. You can hear the sound of **au** and **aw** in **August** and **paw**.

drawing	straws	
lawn	yawn	August
autumn	haul	Paula
pause	crawls	

1. _____ is a lazy month.

2. We _____ in our work to relax.

3. _____ and I play games in the shade.

4. I water the _____ in the evenings.

5. We _____ the picnic basket to the lake.

6. After swimming, we _____ and nap in the sun.

7. We sip lemonade through _____.

8. My baby brother _____ on the grass.

9. Summer's end is _____ near.

10. Soon, _____ will come, and school will start.

Why does this family like August?

Copyright © Savvas Learning Company LLC. All Rights Reserved.

Vowel digraphs au, aw: High-frequency words, critical thinking   **195**

▶ **Find a word in a crayon that will finish each sentence. Print it on the line.**

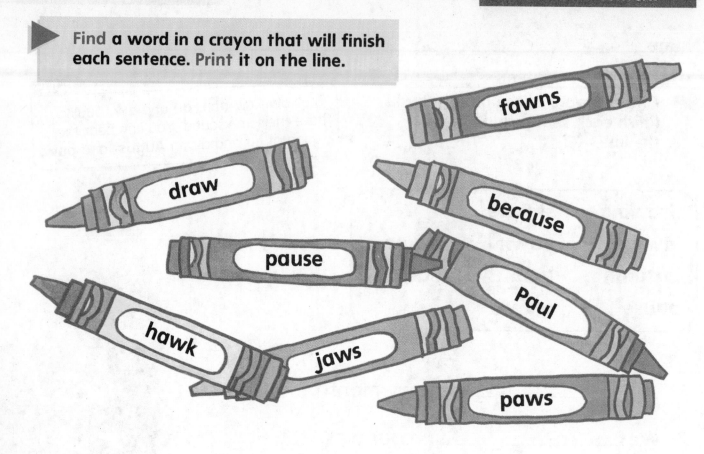

fawns

draw

because

pause

Paul

hawk

jaws

paws

1. After school, _____ likes to draw.

2. When he draws, he doesn't _____.

3. He can _____ any kind of animal.

4. Paul can make a _____ with sharp claws.

5. He can draw a dinosaur with powerful _____.

6. He draws dogs with huge _____.

7. He draws _____ hiding near trees.

8. Paul draws so well _____ he practices a lot.

What other animals might Paul like to draw?

Have your child write a story using one or more of the words on pages 195–196.

Vowel digraphs au, aw: High-frequency words, critical thinking

Name _____

▶ **Read** the words in the bubbles. **Print** each word next to the picture that has the same vowel sound.

cook   haul

broom   hook   head

yawn   claw   pool

boots

bread   heavy   good

1. _____

2. _____

3. _____

4. _____

5. _____

6. _____

7. _____

8. _____

9. _____

10. _____

11. _____

12. _____

Copyright © Savvas Learning Company LLC. All Rights Reserved.

Say the name of each picture. Circle the letters that stand for the vowel sound in the picture's name. Then, print the letters to finish its name. Trace the whole word.

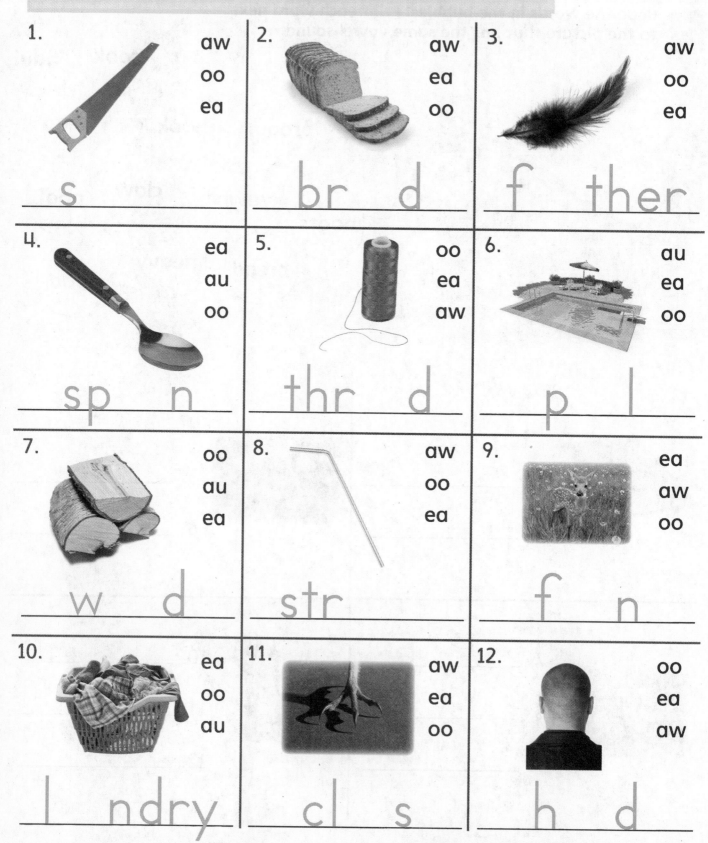

1. aw
   oo
   ea

   s ___

2. aw
   ea
   oo

   br ___ d

3. aw
   oo
   ea

   f ___ ther

4. ea
   au
   oo

   sp ___ n

5. oo
   ea
   aw

   thr ___ d

6. au
   ea
   oo

   p ___ l

7. oo
   au
   ea

   w ___ d

8. aw
   oo
   ea

   str ___

9. ea
   aw
   oo

   f ___ n

10. ea
    oo
    au

    l ___ ndry

11. aw
    ea
    oo

    cl ___ s

12. oo
    ea
    aw

    h ___ d

With your child, make lists of words that rhyme with *saw* and *pool*. Then, check the spelling.

Name _____

Read **the article.** Print **a word with oo, ea, au, or aw from the article on the lines below to finish each sentence.**

Where Are the Dinosaurs?

Long ago, the heavy feet of dinosaurs shook the earth. Then, something awful happened. These awesome animals died. What really happened?

Some scientists think a meteor or comet hit the earth, causing great fires. Dust and ash blocked the sun's light and changed the weather. Warm places became cool. Plants and animals died because of the cold. The dinosaurs could not find food.

Other scientists have taught that the dinosaurs did not disappear, but became other animals as the world changed. If this is true, then they are still with us!

1. The _____ feet of dinosaurs once _____ the earth.

2. A comet may have hit the earth, _____ great fires.

3. These _____ animals have all died.

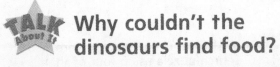

Why couldn't the dinosaurs find food?

Copyright © Savvas Learning Company LLC. All Rights Reserved.

Digraphs oo, ea, au, aw: Critical thinking   **199**

Use **a vowel digraph to complete the words on the tiles. On the lines,** write **each real word you make.**

c _ _ l	b _ _ k	t _ _ p

oo

1. _____

2. _____

y _ _ n	w _ _ d	h _ _ k

aw

3. _____

4. _____

h _ _ d	st _ _ w	br _ _ d

ea

5. _____

6. _____

p _ _ se	m _ _ t	h _ _ l

au

7. _____

8. _____

Write a sentence for one of the words you made.

_____

_____

HOME
With your child, make a word search puzzle using four of the words he or she made.

Where Is My Mother?

The sun shone on a huge egg. The egg shook and began to crack. Soon, a head looked out. "Hmmm," the baby dinosaur thought, "Where is my mother?" He crawled out of the egg and looked around.

1

FOLD

Now, dinosaur was huge. One day he lifted his head, and a smile spread on his face. "Oh my, you are my mother, and you were near me all the time." They paused to snuggle and nibble some branches.

4

Copyright © Savvas Learning Company LLC. All Rights Reserved.

Review vowel digraphs: Take-home book   **201**

Dinosaur looked up, but because he was so small, he saw only grass and strange trees. As he grew, he saw that the trees looked bigger, and the grass looked smaller. Still, he could not find his mother.

2

The strange trees looked very tall now, and they made booming noises. Dinosaur wondered if he would ever find his mother. With his jaws, he ate plants without pausing, and he grew and grew.

3

Name_____

Dino sleeps outside the house.
He never makes a sound.
He doesn't eat the flowers.
He's the greatest pet in town.

▶ **Say the name of the picture. Find its name in the list. Print its letter on the line next to the picture.**

RULE

A **diphthong** is made up of two letters blended together to make one vowel sound. You can hear the sound of the diphthongs **ou** and **ow** in **house** and **flowers**.

1.

_____

2.

_____

3.

_____

4.

_____

a. clown   g. cloud
b. mouse   h. cow
c. shower   i. towel
d. howl   j. flowers
e. owl   k. house
f. crown   l. mouth

5.

_____

6.

_____

7.

_____

8.

_____

9.

_____

10.

_____

Copyright © Savvas Learning Company LLC. All Rights Reserved.

> ▶ **Read each sentence. Circle the ou or ow word in the sentence. Print it on the line.**

1. I live on the edge of a small town. _____

2. My house is near a farm. _____

3. I spend a lot of time outdoors. _____

4. From my yard, I can see cows and horses. _____

5. In the summer, I watch the farmer plow his field. _____

6. His tractor makes a loud noise. _____

7. At night, I hear many different sounds. _____

8. I can hear owls calling. _____

9. I like to watch the clouds beyond the hills. _____

10. In the fall, the flowers on the hill bloom. _____

11. Today, I saw a flock of birds flying south. _____

12. They sense that winter is about to start. _____

 Where does the person telling the story live?

 Ask your child to read the story to you.

Name _____

▶ Find **a word in the box that answers each riddle.** Print **it on the line.**

owl	flower	house	plow
cow	cloud	clown	ground

1. I am in the sky.
   Sometimes I bring you rain.
   What am I?

   _____

2. I wear a funny suit.
   I do many tricks.
   I can make you smile.
   What am I?

   _____

3. I am in the garden.
   I am very colorful.
   I may grow in your yard, too.

   _____

4. You can plant seeds in me.
   The farmer must plow me.
   What am I?

   _____

5. I am wide awake in the dark.
   I hoot and have big eyes.
   What am I?

   _____

6. You can see me at the farm.
   I eat green grass.
   I give you good milk.
   What am I?

   _____

7. You can live in me.
   I will keep you warm and cozy.
   What am I?

   _____

8. The farmer uses me.
   I help him make his garden.
   What am I?

   _____

Copyright © Savvas Learning Company LLC. All Rights Reserved.

RULE

> Remember, **ow** can stand for the long **o** sound, as in **snow,** or it can make a sound of its own, as in **clown.**

▶ **Print an X beside each word in which ow stands for the long o sound.**

1. _____ how   2. _____ snow   3. _____ own   4. _____ town

5. _____ crowd   6. _____ now   7. _____ bowl   8. _____ grow

9. _____ low   10. _____ plow   11. _____ power   12. _____ owl

13. _____ slow   14. _____ flow   15. _____ know   16. _____ show

17. _____ brown   18. _____ crow   19. _____ crown   20. _____ down

21. _____ towel   22. _____ glow   23. _____ throw   24. _____ shower

25. _____ cow   26. _____ blow   27. _____ arrow   28. _____ tower

▶ **Circle the ow word in each sentence. Print an X in the correct column to show which sound ow makes.**

	long vowel	diphthong
29. The circus came to our town.	_____	_____
30. We went to the show last night.	_____	_____
31. We sat in the very first row.	_____	_____
32. The star was a funny clown.	_____	_____
33. He made the crowd laugh.	_____	_____

HOME Help your child make cards for words 1–10 and sort them according to the ow sound.

Name _____

RULE
The diphthongs **oi** and **oy** usually stand for the same sound. You can hear that sound in **coin** and **boy**.

▶ **Circle the name of each picture.**

1.

bow
boil
bill

2.

boy
bag
toy

3.

corn
coil
coins

4.

sail
sell
soil

5.

oak
oil
out

6.

toil
tail
toys

7.

paint
point
pail

8.

noise
nail
nose

9.

fame
foil
fawn

▶ **Finish each sentence with a word from the box.**

enjoy
toy
coins

10. I have saved a few dollars and some _____.

11. I will buy a _____ robot kit.

12. I will _____ putting it together.

Copyright © Savvas Learning Company LLC. All Rights Reserved.

Uncle Roy's Surprise

Uncle Roy asked Troy and his sister Joyce to join him on a surprise trip! Joyce knew where Uncle Roy was taking them, but she did not tell. She did not want to annoy Uncle Roy or spoil the surprise.

Troy was overjoyed when they got to the museum. Both Troy and Joyce enjoyed seeing the dinosaurs. Troy liked *Tyrannosaurus rex*, the king of the meat-eaters, best of all. He could almost hear the noisy roars of its voice.

Uncle Roy told Troy and Joyce that they could choose a toy at the museum's shop. They felt so joyful. Troy's choice was a model of *Tyrannosaurus rex*. He was a very lucky boy!

 Use the words you marked to answer the questions.

1. How did Troy feel when they got to the museum? _____

2. What was Troy's sister's name? _____

3. How did Troy think the dinosaur's roars may have sounded? _____

4. What could Troy and Joyce choose? _____

 What other things could they have seen at the museum?

 Have your child make up his or her own story using some of the words he or she circled or boxed.

Name_____

Find **the word in the box that will finish each sentence.** Print **it on the line.**

spoil	Joy
oil	choice
joins	Floyd's
boy	enjoy
toys	noise

1. Floyd is a hungry _____.

2. He does not want to play with his _____.

3. He would like to _____ a bowl of popcorn.

4. _____ friend Joy wants popcorn, too.

5. Popcorn won't _____ their dinner.

6. Joy _____ Floyd in the kitchen.

7. Floyd pours some _____ in a pot.

8. _____ tells him to be careful.

9. The children listen for a popping _____.

10. Did Floyd and Joy make a good _____?

Do you think they made a good choice? Why?

Diphthongs oi, oy: High-frequency words, critical thinking   **209**

Copyright © Savvas Learning Company LLC. All Rights Reserved.

Find the word in the box that will finish each sentence. Print it on the line.

1. _____ is glad the circus is in town.

2. She loves the _____ of the crowd.

3. The clown rides in a _____ cart.

4. She smiles and _____ at the funny clown.

5. She sees a _____ standing up on a horse.

6. Nothing can _____ the day for Joyce.

7. Joyce always _____ a day at the circus.

| spoil |
| enjoys |
| toy |
| Joyce |
| noise |
| points |
| boy |

 Circle yes or no to answer each question.

8. Is a penny a coin?   Yes   No

9. Is joy being very sad?   Yes   No

10. Can you play with a toy?   Yes   No

11. Is oil used in a car?   Yes   No

12. Is a point the same as paint?   Yes   No

13. Can you boil water?   Yes   No

14. Can you make a choice?   Yes   No

15. Is a loud noise quiet?   Yes   No

With your child, take turns using the *oi* and *oy* words in new sentences.

Name _____

RULE

The diphthong **ew** stands for the long **u** sound. You can hear the long **u** sound in **new** and **few**.

▶ **Find the word in the box that will finish each sentence. Print it on the line.**

grew
blew
chew
flew
stew
new
threw
knew
few

1. I have a _____ pack of sugarless gum.

2. I put a _____ pieces into my mouth.

3. I began to _____ the gum.

4. Then, I _____ a giant bubble.

5. That bubble grew and _____.

6. Suddenly, I _____ I was in trouble.

7. The bubble broke, and pieces _____ everywhere.

8. I _____ the pieces of chewed gum away.

9. I think I will have a warm bowl of _____ instead.

▶ **Print the missing letters for a word that rhymes with each word. Trace the whole word.**

10. few

____st_____

11. crew

____thr_____

12. grew

____fl_____

▶ **Circle** the word that will finish each sentence.

1. (Drew, Blew, Knew) wanted a pet.

2. He went to a pet shop called (crew, dew, Flew) the Coop.

3. He saw puppies (chewing, stewing, mewing) on toy bones.

4. Baby birds (flew, stew, knew) around their cages.

5. They (few, threw, grew) seeds on the floor.

6. Drew really wanted a (mew, stew, new) kitten.

7. He saw a (chew, few, grew) kittens.

8. One (chewed, threw, grew) its food.

9. Another kitten saw him and (flew, mewed, chewed).

10. Drew (grew, dew, knew) he wanted that kitten.

11. Drew named his kitten (Mews, Stews, Dews) because it always mewed.

12. That kitten (new, grew, chew) bigger every day.

13. Mews liked it when Drew (few, threw, mew) a toy to him.

14. He liked to (chew, new, stew) on Drew's shoelaces.

15. Mews tried to hide under the (screws, grew, newspaper).

16. From the window he watched birds as they (flew, crew, dew).

17. When the wind (blew, drew, stew), Mews chased fallen leaves.

18. He licked drops of morning (mew, dew, chew).

19. Before Drew (threw, few, knew) it, Mews was his friend.

20. Drew really loved his (stew, new, flew) pet.

 What do you think Drew liked best about Mews?

 With your child, take turns reading sentences from the story.

Name _____

Say and spell the words in the box. Name each picture and write each word whose name has the same vowel sound. Then, circle the letters that stand for the vowel sound.

owl	rain	seed	wealth	lie	tray
coat	cool	draw	boy	food	house
pie	spoil	hoe	bean	haul	head

1.

_____
_____

2.

_____
_____

3.

_____
_____

4.

_____
_____

5.

_____
_____

6.

_____
_____

7.
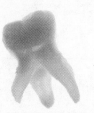
_____
_____

8.

_____
_____

9.

_____
_____

Review vowel pairs, digraphs, diphthongs   **213**

When you write a **free-verse poem**, you can use colorful words to describe something or tell how you feel. Rhyming words are not used in a free-verse poem. The writer says a lot in a few words.

▶ Write a free-verse poem about dinosaurs. Use some of the words in the box. Share your poem with the class.

look	tail	noise	claw	tie
ready	meat	found	toe	few
day	eat	green	die	new

Use colorful words to tell about dinosaurs.

Do not use rhyming words.

_____

_____

_____

_____

_____

_____

_____

_____

214 Vowel pairs, digraphs, diphthongs

 Invite your child to read his or her poem aloud to family members.

Best-Loved Dinosaur Riddles

1. What do you call dinosaur fossils that sleep until noon?

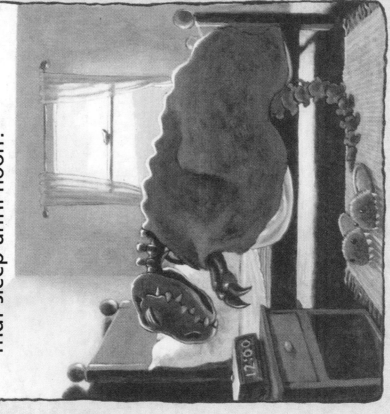

1. lazy-bones

---

6. What do you call a goofy dinosaur?

7. On what side of a dinosaur's house should he plant a tree?

6. a silly-osaurus   7. on the outside

Review vowel pairs, digraphs, diphthongs: Take-home book   **215**

2. How did the dinosaur find the missing train?

3. What do you call a triceratops that fell down?

2. He followed the tracks!   3. A dino-sore

2

- - - - - - FOLD - - - - - -

4. What do dinosaurs drink from in outer space?

5. Why do the boys and girls enjoy playing with the dinosaur?

4. flying saucers   5. It is tons of fun.

3

Name _____

Circle **the word that will finish each sentence. Then,** print **it on the line.**

1. A baby deer is a _____.　　seal　fawn　feather

2. Green _____ are good to eat.　　beans　baits　bowls

3. A place where you can see animals is a _____.　　zoo　zipper　hook

4. Dried grass that horses eat is _____.　　seed　hay　day

5. A small animal with a long tail is a _____.　　men　mitt　mouse

6. Something you row is a _____.　　boat　beach　boy

7. You walk on your two _____.　　feet　foot　flat

8. One animal that gives milk is a _____.　　cloud　crow　cow

9. Something that was never used is _____.　　grew　new　draw

10. A dish under a cup is a _____.　　train　faucet　saucer

Copyright © Savvas Learning Company LLC. All Rights Reserved.

Vowel pairs, digraphs, diphthongs: Assessment　　**217**

Fill in **the bubble in front of the word that will finish each sentence.**

1. Dinosaurs ___ their eggs in nests. ○ laid ○ paid

2. The mother ___ around the eggs. ○ coiled ○ boiled

3. Many dinosaurs ___ huge. ○ saw ○ grew

4. The giant tyrannosaurus ate ___. ○ meet ○ meat

5. It had a long claw on each ___. ○ toe ○ foe

6. It had a large ___. ○ bread ○ head

7. It caught animals in its strong ___. ○ jaws ○ hauls

8. The allosaurus had very sharp ___. ○ teeth ○ seeds

9. It had bony spikes on its ___. ○ sail ○ tail

10. No dinosaurs are alive ___. ○ now ○ cow

11. They ___ long ago. ○ died ○ lied

12. We can only guess what they ___ like. ○ looked ○ playing

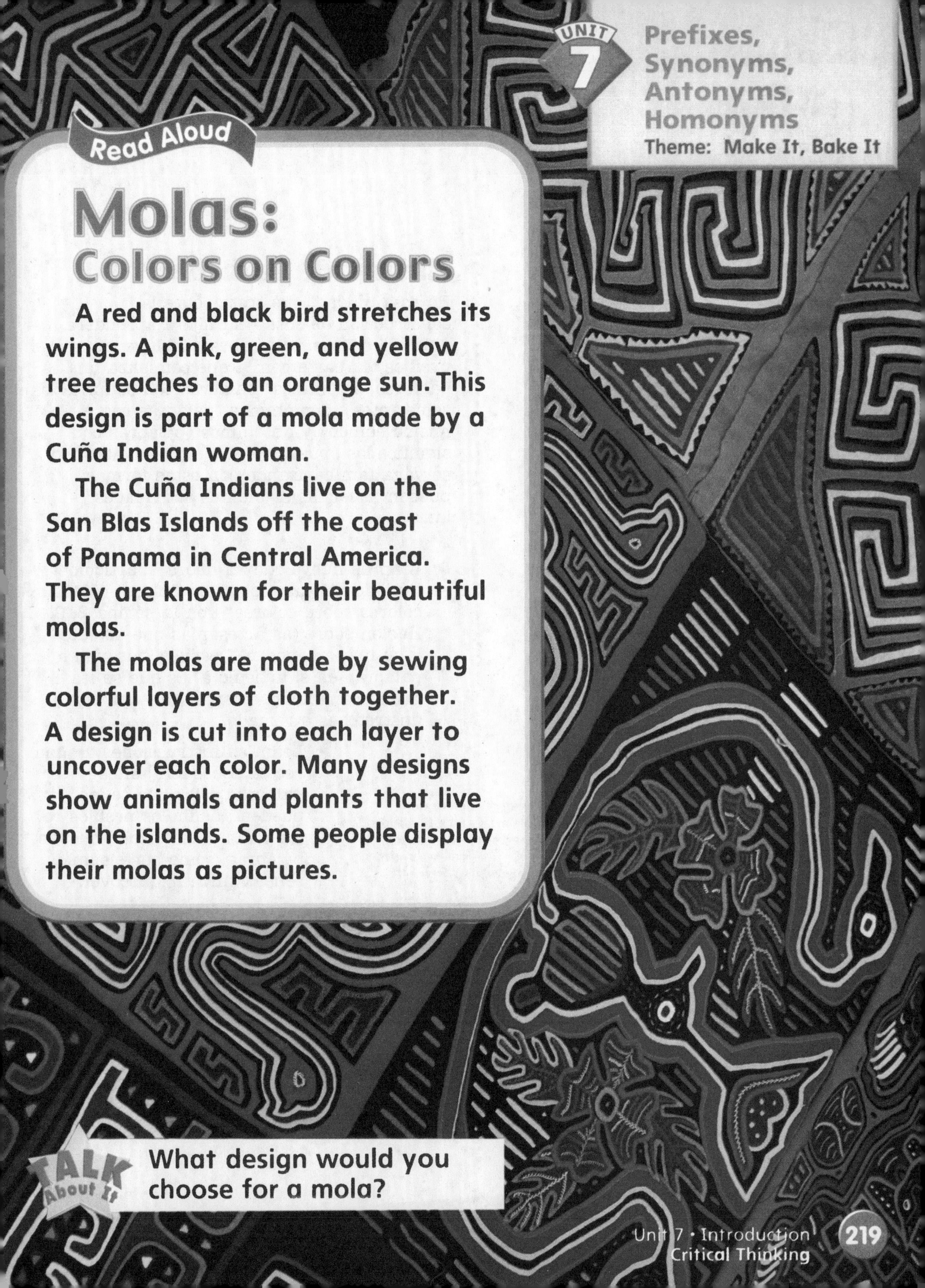

Read Aloud

Molas:
Colors on Colors

A red and black bird stretches its wings. A pink, green, and yellow tree reaches to an orange sun. This design is part of a mola made by a Cuña Indian woman.

The Cuña Indians live on the San Blas Islands off the coast of Panama in Central America. They are known for their beautiful molas.

The molas are made by sewing colorful layers of cloth together. A design is cut into each layer to uncover each color. Many designs show animals and plants that live on the islands. Some people display their molas as pictures.

TALK About It

What design would you choose for a mola?

Dear Family,

In this unit about making things, your child will learn about prefixes (word parts that begin words), synonyms (words with similar meanings), homonyms (words that sound alike), and antonyms (words with opposite meanings). As your child becomes familiar with these forms, you might try these activities together.

► With your child, reread the article "Molas: Colors on Colors" on page 219. Talk about the crafts you and your child are familiar with. Then, find words in the article to which the prefixes **re** and **un** can be added, such as unstretches or remade.

► Read the directions for a recipe. Together, look for words to which the prefixes **re**, **un**, and **dis** can be added to make new words—for example: reheat, unwrap, discover.

To (make) (mashed) potatoes, (place) (peeled) potatoes in a pot with water. (Cover) the pot and (cook) on low (heat.) When (done,) (add) milk, salt and pepper, and (mash) the potatoes. (Serve) hot with butter.

You and your child might enjoy reading these books together.

Easy Origami
By Dokuohtei Nakano

The Button Box
by Margarette S. Reid

Sincerely,

Estimada familia:

En esta unidad, que trata sobre la construcción de cosas, su hijo/a aprenderá diferentes tipos de palabras, incluyendo prefijos (la parte con la que comienza una palabra), sinónimos (palabras con significados semejantes), homónimos (palabras con el mismo sonido) y antónimos (palabras con significados opuestos). A medida que su hijo/a se vaya familiarizando con estas formas, pueden hacer las siguientes actividades juntos.

► Lean de nuevo con su hijo/a el artículo titulado "Molas: Colors on Colors" ("Molas: colores sobre colores") en la página 219. Hablen sobre las artesanías que ustedes y su hijo/a conocen. Después, busquen palabras en el artículo a las que se les pueden añadir los prefijos **re** y **un**, como unstretches o remade.

► Lean las instrucciones de una receta. Busquen juntos palabras a las que se les pueden añadir los prefijos **re**, **un** y **dis** para formar nuevas palabras, como por ejemplo, reheat, unwrap, discover.

► Ustedes y su hijo/a disfrutarán leyendo estos libros juntos.

Easy Origami de Dokuohtei Nakano
The Button Box de Margarette S. Reid

Sinceramente,

Copyright © Savvas Learning Company LLC. All Rights Reserved.

Name _____

Don't throw out old puppets.
Recycle them instead!
Just reglue the hair and eyes,
And then reuse the head.

> Add **re** to the word beside each sentence. **Use the new words to finish the sentences.**

> **RULE**
> The prefix **re** usually means **do again.** Add **re** to the base word **glue** to make **reglue.**
> **Reglue** the hair and eyes.

1. Every day I do things that I have to _____. | **do**

2. When I get up, I _____ my bed. | **make**

3. I _____ my teeth after I eat. | **brush**

4. I _____ my backpack before school. | **pack**

5. I _____ my shoes. | **tie**

6. When my camera needs film, I _____ it. | **load**

7. I read and _____ my favorite books. | **read**

8. I write and _____ my stories. | **write**

9. Every night I _____ my alarm clock. | **wind**

 What things do you redo every day?

Copyright © Savvas Learning Company LLC. All Rights Reserved.

▶ **Add un to the word beside each sentence. Use the new words to finish the sentences.**

> **RULE**
> The prefix **un** means the opposite of the original word. Add **un** to the base word **lock** to make **unlock**.
> The key **unlocks** the door.

1. Every day we do things and _____ them.

2. We dress and _____.

3. We button and _____ our clothes.

4. We tie our shoes and then _____ them.

5. We lock and _____ doors.

6. We buckle our seat belts and _____ them.

7. We wrap up our lunches and then

   _____ them.

8. We pack our backpacks and _____ them.

9. We load film in a camera and later _____ it.

10. I am not _____ about all this undoing.

11. It just seems a little _____ to me.

12. It's probably _____ things will ever change.

do
dress
button
tie
lock
buckle
wrap
pack
load
happy
usual
likely

HOME With your child, take turns making up new sentences for the *un-* words.

Name_____

> Add **re** or **un** to the word beside each sentence.
> Use **the new word to finish the sentence.**

1. Last night my baby sister _____ my backpack.

   `packed`

2. She tried to _____ my homework with her crayon.

   `do`

3. I had to _____ my story.

   `write`

4. Now, I _____ my backpack every night.

   `check`

5. I am very _____ about it.

   `happy`

6. My things are _____ around my sister.

   `safe`

> Print **one word that means the same as each pair of words.**

7. not cooked _____

8. not safe _____

9. not able _____

10. not kind _____

11. spell again _____

12. use again _____

13. play again _____

14. tell again _____

Copyright © Savvas Learning Company LLC. All Rights Reserved.

> Add the prefix **un** or **re** to each underlined word. Print the new word on the line.

1. to <u>read</u> again

_____

2. opposite of <u>lock</u>

_____

3. to <u>fill</u> again

_____

4. opposite of <u>tie</u>

_____

5. opposite of <u>buckle</u>

_____

6. to <u>heat</u> again

_____

7. to <u>build</u> again

_____

8. opposite of <u>pack</u>

_____

9. to <u>write</u> again

_____

10. opposite of <u>happy</u>

_____

11. to <u>play</u> again

_____

12. to <u>wind</u> again

_____

 HOME

Write prefixes (re-, un-) and base words on separate cards. Match them to make new words.

Name _____

Add **dis** to the word beside each sentence. **Use the new words to finish the sentences.**

RULE
The prefix **dis** also means the opposite of the original word. Add **dis** to the base word **order** to make **disorder**.

1. My shoe _____ again. **appeared**

2. I _____ that it was missing. **liked**

3. "Why did you _____ me, Wags?" **obey**

4. "You know I'm _____ when you take my things." **pleased**

5. "That was a _____ thing to do." **loyal**

6. "Wags, you are a _____." **grace**

7. Wags barked to _____. **agree**

8. He pulled my shoe out of my

_____ toy chest. **orderly**

 What did the boy think happened to his shoe?

Copyright © Savvas Learning Company LLC. All Rights Reserved.

Fill in **the bubble beside the word that will finish each sentence.** Write **the word on the line.**

1. Mr. Fixit will

_____

the telephone before fixing it.

- ○ discolor
- ○ disconnect

2. The rider will

_____

and let her horse rest.

- ○ dismount
- ○ distaste

3. Meg and Peg are twin sisters, but

they _____
about many things.

- ○ disagree
- ○ disappear

4. The puppy

_____ its
owner and ran outside with her hat.

- ○ dishonest
- ○ disobeyed

5. John loves green beans, but he

_____

eggplant.

- ○ dislikes
- ○ disgrace

6. Kirk made the dirt appear, so he
had to make it

_____.

- ○ disappear
- ○ distrust

226 Prefix dis-

Name _____

> Add **un**, **dis**, or **re** to each base word to make a new word. Print the word on the line.

un or **dis**		**re** or **dis**	
1. _____ agree	2. _____ happy	7. _____ able	8. _____ writes
3. _____ obey	4. _____ easy	9. _____ new	10. _____ like
5. _____ lucky	6. _____ please	11. _____ pay	12. _____ loyal

> Add **un**, **dis**, or **re** to each underlined word to change the meaning of the sentence. Print the new word on the line.

13. Grandpa was <u>pleased</u> about the plans for his party. _____

14. He said he felt <u>easy</u> about getting gifts. _____

15. Sadly, Sue <u>wrapped</u> the present she had made. _____

16. Then, Jake said they would <u>obey</u> Grandpa just once. _____

17. With a grin, Sue <u>wrapped</u> the gift. _____

18. She <u>tied</u> the bow. _____

19. Grandpa was not <u>happy</u> with his party after all. _____

Copyright © Savvas Learning Company LLC. All Rights Reserved.

Draw a line from the prefix to a base word to make a new word. Write the word on the line.

un	write
dis	happy
re	obey

1. _____

2. _____

3. _____

dis	easy
re	agree
un	pay

4. _____

5. _____

6. _____

▶ **Add re, un, or dis to the base word to make a word that will finish the sentence. Write the new word on the line.**

7.	Amber will _____ the gift.	wrap
8.	Alex and Max _____.	agree
9.	Rita will _____ the house.	build
10.	Taro is never _____ to animals.	kind
11.	Look! The ice is still _____.	safe
12.	My baby sister _____ rice.	likes
13.	The magician made the bird _____.	appear

HOME

Have your child use the new words in the boxes at the top of the page in sentences.

Name _____

The gifts and presents are wrapped.
It's easy and simple to do.
Little and small, big and large,
Here's a box for you!

RULE

Synonyms are words that have the same or almost the same meaning. **Gifts** and **presents** mean the same thing.

▶ Print **each word from the box beside a word that means the same thing.**

1. big _____   2. small _____

3. happy _____   4. quick _____

5. sick _____   6. jump _____

| glad |
| ill |
| leap |
| fast |
| little |
| large |

▶ Circle **the word in each row that means the same as the first word.**

7. **jolly**	sad	big	happy	jump
8. **junk**	gems	trash	list	top
9. **pile**	heap	near	rest	stop
10. **sleep**	awake	nap	paint	read
11. **sick**	ill	quick	lazy	glad
12. **quick**	step	slow	pony	fast
13. **sound**	sad	noise	find	happy
14. **large**	huge	many	tiny	blue
15. **close**	move	let	shut	see

Copyright © Savvas Learning Company LLC. All Rights Reserved.

Finish **Peggy's** letter. **Print** a word from the box that means the same thing as the word below each line.

friend	kind	big
gifts	laugh	little
noise	happy	enjoy
fast	races	
hope	easy	

May 10

Dear Pablo,

    I'm _____ that you came to my party.

              glad

It was _____ of you to bring _____.

         nice   presents

The _____ book looks _____ to read.

        large   simple

I will _____ reading it. When I wind up the

       like

_____ robot, it _____ _____

  small   runs   quickly

and makes a funny _____. It makes me

                      sound

_____ to watch it. Thank you very much.

  giggle

I _____ to see you soon.

    wish

                         Your _____,

                                  pal

                         Peggy

Why did Peggy write to Pablo?

Ask your child to read Peggy's letter to you.

Name _____

Hot or cold, rain or shine,
My dog likes the backyard best.
Day or night, summer or winter,
He needs a place to rest.

▶ Find **a word in the box that means the opposite of each word. Print its letter on the line.**

RULE

Antonyms are words that are opposite or almost opposite in meaning. **Hot** and **cold** mean the opposite of each other.

a. **old**	b. **wet**	c. **start**	d. **full**	e. **slow**
f. **last**	g. **down**	h. **hot**	i. **good**	j. **short**
k. **out**	l. **well**	m. **few**	n. **winter**	o. **long**
p. **far**	q. **lower**	r. **shallow**	s. **shut**	t. **awake**
u. **thick**	v. **wide**	w. **white**	x. **hard**	

1. ____ dry   2. ____ up   3. ____ summer   4. ____ short

5. ____ near   6. ____ fast   7. ____ tall   8. ____ bad

9. ____ cold   10. ____ thin   11. ____ sick   12. ____ many

13. ____ stop   14. ____ upper   15. ____ first   16. ____ deep

17. ____ new   18. ____ empty   19. ____ open   20. ____ in

21. ____ asleep   22. ____ easy   23. ____ black   24. ____ narrow

Copyright © Savvas Learning Company LLC. All Rights Reserved.

Print a word from the box that means the opposite of each word and describes the picture.

stop	open	full	ill	cry	night
float	hot	strong	asleep	sit	smile

1. awake

_____

2. close

_____

3. empty

_____

4. cold

_____

5. healthy

_____

6. stand

_____

7. weak

_____

8. sink

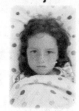

_____

9. day

_____

10. laugh

_____

11. frown

_____

12. go

_____

 With your child, take turns using each antonym pair in a sentence.

Name_____

Grandma will sew a blue-green quilt
So everyone can see,
How the wind blew the boats about
On a stormy day at sea.

RULE

Homonyms are words that sound alike but have different spellings and meanings. **Blue** and **blew** are homonyms.

▶ Find **a word in the box that sounds the same as each word below.** Print **the word on the line.**

tail	here	to	road	pail	heal
blue	week	cent	sail	maid	sea

1. heel _____

2. see _____

3. rode _____

4. sent _____

5. tale _____

6. blew _____

7. weak _____

8. pale _____

9. hear _____

10. two _____

11. sale _____

12. made _____

▶ Circle **the word that will finish each sentence.** Print **it on the line.**

13. Maggie _____ her horse into the woods.   road   rode

14. Her puppy wagged its _____ and ran along.   tail   tale

15. They saw a _____ hidden behind a tree.   dear   deer

16. Maggie watched the _____ set in the west.   son   sun

Copyright © Savvas Learning Company LLC. All Rights Reserved.

Find **a word in the box that sounds the same as each word below. Print it on the line.**

rose	meat	blew	too	pane
tow	tale	week	four	wait
beet	bare	sea	dear	sew

1. weight _____
2. rows _____
3. weak _____

4. bear _____
5. blue _____
6. beat _____

7. deer _____
8. two _____
9. for _____

10. pain _____
11. see _____
12. meet _____

13. so _____
14. tail _____
15. toe _____

Use **words from the box and the activity above to finish the sentences.**

16. Pete bought a new kite last _____.

17. He could not _____ to try it out.

18. He could _____ his friends playing outside.

19. He pulled on his _____ jeans in a hurry.

20. He wanted to fly his kite _____.

Help your child write each homonym on a card or paper and then match them.

Name _____

Read **the words in the box. Then,** write **two words that belong under each heading.**

Words That Mean the Same Thing

_____ _____

Words That Sound the Same

_____ _____

Words That Are Opposites

_____ _____

Words That Begin with dis

_____ _____

Words That Begin with un

_____ _____

Words That Begin with re

_____ _____

rewrite
dislike
hot
little
reread
undo
cold
deer
dear
disagree
unhappy
small

Copyright © Savvas Learning Company LLC. All Rights Reserved.

Prefixes, synonyms, antonyms, homonyms   **235**

A **set of instructions** are written to tell how to make or do something. The writer tells what the instructions are for, and lists the materials that are needed. Then, the steps needed to follow the directions are written in order and numbered.

▶ Write **a** set of instructions **telling how to make your favorite sandwich. Use some of the words in the box to help you.**

unwrap	recover	two	to	top
bottom	dislike	slice	piece	reuse

Tell what the instructions are for.

_____

_____

List what is needed.

_____

_____

Tell the steps in order and number them.

_____

_____

_____

_____

_____

HOME With your child, create another *set of instructions* for making or doing something.

Make Your Own Clay Dough

You can make your own clay dough. It is easy and simple to do. This is what you need:

2 cups salt   5 cups flour
2 cups warm water   food coloring

1

Let the shapes you made dry if you wish to keep them. You may choose to reuse the dough when you are done. Then, store it in the refrigerator in a plastic container to keep it wet. Remember to have fun!

4

Mix the salt, flour, and water. Refill the cup and add more water if you need it. Knead and reknead the dough until it is smooth and even. Use food coloring if you wish to color the dough.

2

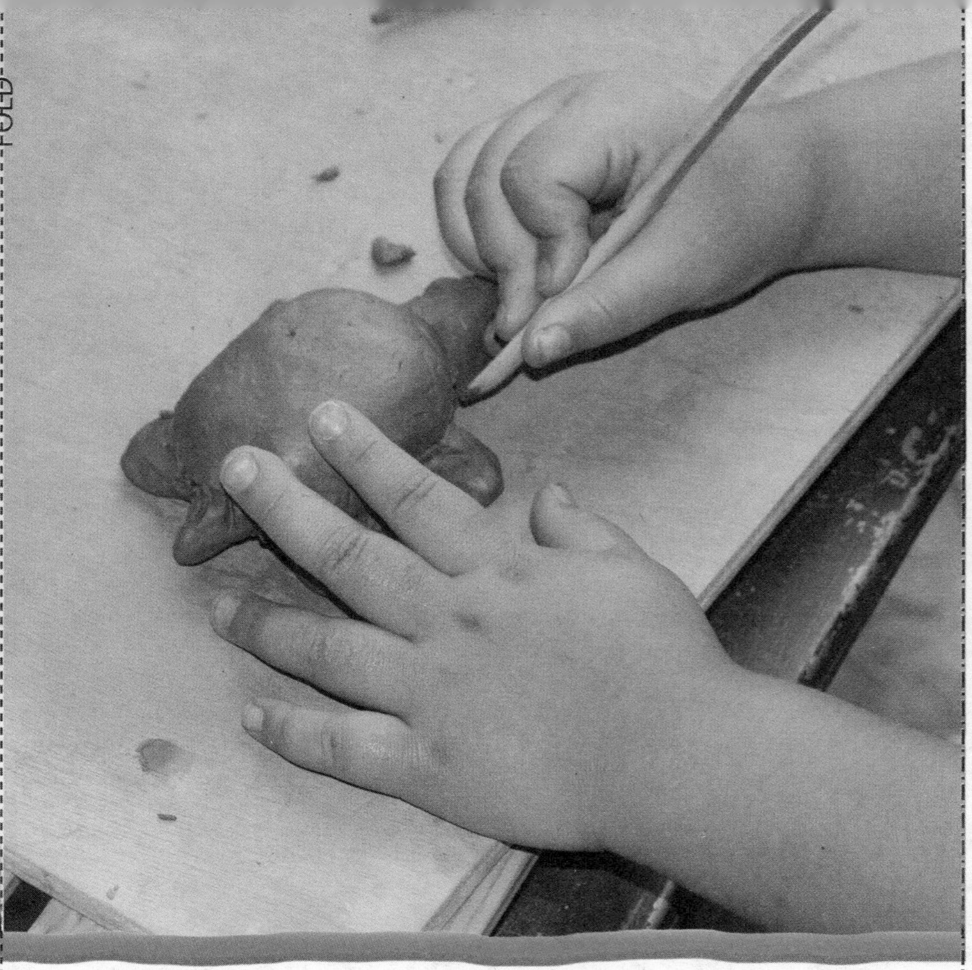

Roll out the dough. Don't make it too thick or too thin. You can mold the dough, or you can cut out your favorite shapes. They can be big or little, tall or short.

3

238   Prefixes, synonyms, antonyms, homonyms: Take-home book

Name _____

> Circle two words in each box that mean the same thing.

1. cold cool	2. hair small	3. fast fell
seed shook	little home	quick queen
4. three tree	5. jump leap	6. sick snow
shut close	drink drop	ill blow

> Circle two words in each box that mean the opposite.

7. little puppy	8. fly old	9. bad candy
jelly big	new penny	rich good
10. they fast	11. from dirty	12. asleep play
play slow	clean funny	baby awake

> Circle the word that will finish each sentence. Print it on the line.

13. The _____ was shining.   sun   son

14. I put on my _____ shorts and blue hat.   read   red

15. I went for a sail on the _____.   see   sea

16. The wind blew the _____.   sails   sales

17. It almost _____ my hat off, too.   blew   blue

18. I had a _____ time!   grate   great

Copyright © Savvas Learning Company LLC. All Rights Reserved.

> **Fill in the bubble beside the word that names or describes each picture.**

1.
- ○ tale
- ○ tell
- ○ tail

2.
- ○ heel
- ○ hail
- ○ heal

3.
- ○ day
- ○ deer
- ○ dear

4.
- ○ rode
- ○ rod
- ○ road

5.
- ○ sun
- ○ son
- ○ soon

6.
- ○ knows
- ○ nose
- ○ now

> **Read the words. Fill in the bubble next to the word that has the same meaning.**

7. opposite of wrap
- ○ unwrap
- ○ rewrap

8. to play again
- ○ replay
- ○ display

9. opposite of mount
- ○ dismount
- ○ remount

10. opposite of appear
- ○ reappear
- ○ disappear

11. spell again
- ○ dispell
- ○ respell

12. to tie again
- ○ untie
- ○ retie

13. opposite of like
- ○ dislike
- ○ relike

14. opposite of do
- ○ redo
- ○ undo

15. to pack again
- ○ repack
- ○ unpack

240 Prefixes, synonyms, antonyms, homonyms: Assessment

Phonics

LEVEL B   Elwell • Murray • Kucia

ILLUSTRATIONS: Page 112: Anthony Accardo. 35, 36, 77, 78, 89: Elizabeth Allen. 45: Gary Bialke. 92, 163, 208: Denny Bond. 122: Cindy Brodie. 203: Annette Cable. 4, 192: Chi Chung. 225: Daniel Clifford. 11: Chris Demarest. 22: Shelley Dieterich. 3, 133, 153, 233: Karen Dugan. 42: Julie Durrell. 44, 131, 210, 228: Len Ebert. 150, 165, 234: Kate Flanagan. 41: Rusty Fletcher. 90, 226: Toni Goffe. 117, 118: Renee Graef. 231: Gershom Griffith. 88: Pat Dewitt Grush. 91, 101, 119, 135: Meryl Henderson. 126: Steve Henry. 51, 52: Kathryn Hewitt. 1, 2, 63, 67, 105, 201, 202: Dennis Hockerman. 196: Claude Martinot. 31, 97, 164, 229: Meredith Johnson. 49, 50: Holly Jones. 157: Ron Jones. 123: Wallace Keller. 103, 223: Anne Kennedy. 132, 148: Terry Kovalcik. 73, 137: Jeff Le Van. 160, 230: Jason Levinson. 107: Anthony Lewis. 215, 216: Brian Lies. 109, 191: Diana Magnuson. 39: Claude Martinot. 26, 46: Anni Matsick. 1, 27: Erin Mauterer. 28, 159: Patrick Merrell. 4, 181, 235: Judith Moffatt. 95: Susan Nethery. 43, 87, 125: Christina Ong. 221: L.S. Pierce. 147, 167, 195: Francesc Rovira. 23: Ellen Sasaki. 179: Stacey Schuett. 93, 187: D.J. Simison. 55: Susan Swan. 113, 212: Maggie Swanson. 57: Terry Taylor. 59: George Ulrich. 94, 111, 156: Gary Undercuffler. 64: Bruce Van Patter. 197: Thor Wickstrom. 47, 48, 145: Amy Wummer. 155, 168: Lane Yerkes. 2, 134: Jerry Zimmerman.

ACKNOWLEDGMENTS: "Something Big Has Been Here" by Jack Prelutsky. Text copyright © 1990 by Jack Prelutsky. Illustrations copyright © 1990 by Jack Stevenson. Used by permission of HarperCollins Publishers. "The Folk Who Live in Backward Town" by Mary Ann Hoberman. Reprinted by permission of Harcourt, Inc. Reprinted by permission of Gina Maccoby Literary Agency in the British Commonwealth. Copyright © 1959, renewed 1987, 1998 by Mary Ann Hoberman. "Taking Off" by Mary McB.Green from *The 20th Century Children's Poetry Tresury* selected by Jack Prelutsky © 1999, illustrated by Meilo So © 1999.

NOTE: Every effort has been made to locate the copyright owner of material reprinted in this book. Omissions brought to our attention will be corrected in subsequent printings.

PHOTOGRAPHS: Cover: © Eric Isselee/Shutterstock. Page 7: *bmr.* © Anatoliy Meshkov/Fotolia, *tml.* © Victoria Liu/Fotolia, *mtl.* © Petr Masek/Fotolia, *mbl.* © Getty Images/Hemera Technologies/Thinkstock, *mbml.* © StarJumper/Fotolia, *mbr.* © Getty Images/Thinkstock, *tl.* © Thomas Northcut/Thinkstock, *tmr.* © Stockbyte/Thinkstock, *tr.* © Stockbyte/Thinkstock, *mtr.* © James Steidl/Fotolia, *mtmr.* © Aleksandr Ugorenkov/Fotolia, *mtr.* © Brand X Pictures/Thinkstock, *mbmr.* © Hemera Technologies/Thinkstock, *bl.* © Borys Shevchuk/Fotolia, *bml.* © Oneuser/Fotolia, *br.* © Iznogood/Fotolia. 8: *mbmr.* © Yxowert/Fotolia, *tml.* © DC Productions/Thinkstock, *mtmr.* © Yui/Fotolia, *mtr.* © Birgit Kutzera/Fotolia, *mbl.* © Jupiterimages/Thinkstock, *mbml.* © Eray/Fotolia, *bml.* © Hemera Technologies/Thinkstock, *tl.* © Getty Images/Jupiterimages/Thinkstock, *tr.* © Carl Subick/Fotolia, *mtl.* © PhotoGraPHie/Fotolia, *mbr.* © Blaz Kure/Fotolia, *mbr.* © WINIKI/Fotolia, *bl.* © Iryna Volina/Fotolia, *br.* © Stockbyte/Thinkstock, *br.* © Iosif Szasz-Fabian/Fotolia, *tmr.* © Elaine Barker/Fotolia. 9: *mbr.* © Yxowert/Fotolia, *tmr.* © Jupiterimages/Thinkstock, *mtl.* © Tschmittjohn/Fotolia, *tl.* © Stockbyte/Thinkstock, *tml.* © Stockbyte/Thinkstock, *tr.* © Hemera Technologies/Thinkstock, *mtml.* © imrek/Fotolia, *mtmr.* © Svyatoslav Lypynskyy/Fotolia, *mtr.* © Kasoga/Fotolia, *mbml.* © Berean/Fotolia, *mbmr.* © Comstock/Thinkstock, *bl.* © r-o-x-o-r/Fotolia, *bml.* © WINIKI/Fotolia, *bmr.* © Mikko Pitkänen/Fotolia, *br.* © Rtimages/Fotolia, *mbr.* © Atropat/Fotolia. 10: *bmr.* © Roger Scott/Fotolia, *tml.* © Hemera Technologies/Thinkstock, *mtl.* © Linous/Fotolia, *tl.* © Iryna Volina/Fotolia, *tmr.* © Close Encounters/Fotolia, *tr.* © Thinkstock, *mtml.* © Getty Images/Hemera Technologies/Thinkstock, *mtr.* © Michael Kempf/Fotolia, *mbl.* © Sergik/Fotolia, *mbml.* © Solodovnikova Elena/Fotolia, *mbmr.* © Stockbyte/Thinkstock, *mbr.* © Michael Flippo/Fotolia, *bl.* © Lasse Kristensen/Fotolia, *bml.* © Coprid/Fotolia, *br.* © Lasse Kristensen/Fotolia, *mtmr.* © Elaine Barker/Fotolia. 12: *mtl.* © Hemera Technologies/Thinkstock, *mbl.* © DC Productions/Thinkstock, *mbm.* © Jupiterimages/Thinkstock, *tl.* © Close Encounters/Fotolia, *tm.* © Nbriam/Fotolia, *tr.* © Maksym Gorpenyuk/Thinkstock, *mtm.* © r-o-x-o-r/Fotolia, *mtr.* © Olga Sapegina/Fotolia, *mbr.* © Thinkstock, *bl.* © Picture Partners/Fotolia, *bm.* © Hemera Technologies/Thinkstock, *br.* © Iznogood/Fotolia. 13: *mtmr.* © George Doyle/Thinkstock, *mbml.* © Konstantin Kikvidze/Fotolia, *br.* © Johnaalex/Fotolia, *tl.* © Getty Images/Hemera Technologies/Thinkstock, *tml.* © Hemera Technologies/Thinkstock, *tmr.* © VanHart/Fotolia, *tr.* © Zedcor Wholly Owned/Thinkstock, *mtr.* © Jupiterimages/Thinkstock, *mtml.* © Brand X Pictures/Thinkstock, *mtr.* © Stockbyte/Thinkstock, *mbl.* © Thomas Northcut/Thinkstock, *mbmr.* © Les Cunliffe/Fotolia, *mbr.* © GIS/Fotolia, *bl.* © Akiyoko/Fotolia, *bml.* © Brand X Pictures/Thinkstock, *bmr.* © Tommy/Fotolia. 14: *tr.* © Bayou Jeff/Fotolia, *ml.* © Johnaalex/Fotolia, *br.* © Konstantin Kikvidze/Fotolia, *tl.* © Joss/Fotolia, *mr.* © Comstock/Thinkstock, *bl.* © Iznogood/Fotolia. 17: *t.* © Jupiterimages/Thinkstock, *b.* © ArTo/Fotolia. 18: *t.* © Christophe MONIN/Fotolia, *b.* © Superstock. 19: *tl.* © Petr Masek/Fotolia, *tr.* © Spencer Berger/Fotolia, *ml.* © Tschmittjohn/Fotolia, *bl.* © EyeMark/Fotolia, *tml.* © Dleonis/Fotolia, *tmr.* © Getty Images/Hemera Technologies/Thinkstock, *mmr.* © Close Encounters/Fotolia, *mr.* © Stockbyte/Thinkstock, *bml.* © Iryna Volina/Fotolia, *bmr.* © GIS/Fotolia, *br.* © Irochka/Fotolia, *br.* © Getty Images/Hemera Technologies/Thinkstock. 21: *background.* © Corinne Bertschmann/Superstock. 23: *mr.* © Ayupov Evgeniy/Fotolia, *bm.* © Stockbyte/Thinkstock, *br.* © Jupiterimages/Thinkstock, *tl.* © Thomas Northcut/Thinkstock, *tm.* © Hemera Technologies/Thinkstock, *tr.* © Oneuser/Fotolia, *ml.* © Rtimages/Fotolia, *m.* © Blaz Kure/Fotolia, *bl.* © Iryna Volina/Fotolia. 25: *tl.* © Dick Luria/Thinkstock, *tr.* © Amos Morgan/Thinkstock, *bl.* © Jupiterimages/Thinkstock, *br.* © Aidon/Thinkstock. 27: *m.* © DC Productions/Thinkstock, *mr.* © Hemera Technologies/Thinkstock, *tl.* © Jiri Hera/Fotolia, *tm.* © Ablestock.com/Thinkstock, *tr.* © Getty Images/Hemera Technologies/Thinkstock, *bm.* © Comstock/Thinkstock, *br.* © Melking/Fotolia, *ml.* © Hellen/Fotolia, *bl.* © Iznogood/Fotolia. 29: *tr.* © Hemera Technologies/Thinkstock, *mml.* © DC Productions/Thinkstock, *bml.* © Comstock/Thinkstock, *tml.* © Getty Images/Hemera Technologies/Thinkstock, *tmr.* © Lasse Kristensen/Fotolia, *ml.* © Comstock/Thinkstock, *mmr.* © Melking/Fotolia, *mr.* © PhotoGraPHie/Fotolia, *bmr.* © aris sanjaya/Fotolia, *tl.* © Iznogood/Fotolia, *bl.* © Hellen/Fotolia. 30: *tl.* © Victoria Liu/Fotolia, *ml.* © Hemera Technologies/Thinkstock, *mr.* © DC Productions/Thinkstock, *tm.* © Jiri Hera/Fotolia, *m.* © Getty Images/Hemera Technologies/Thinkstock, *bl.* © PhotoGraPHie/Fotolia, *bm.* © Comstock/Thinkstock, *br.* © Ablestock.com/Thinkstock, *tr.* © Iznogood/Fotolia. 31: *tr.* © Abderit99/Fotolia, *mr.* © Yxowert/Fotolia, *tl.* © Getty Images/Hemera Technologies/Thinkstock, *tm.* © r-o-x-o-r/Fotolia, *ml.* © Blaz Kure/Fotolia, *m.* © Michael Kempf/Fotolia, *bl.* © Maksym Gorpenyuk/Thinkstock, *br.* © Hemera Technologies/Thinkstock, *bm.* © Elaine Barker/Fotolia. 32: *tm.* © Miguel Pinheiro/Fotolia, *tr.* © Yxowert/Fotolia, *mtl.* © Lisa Turay/Fotolia, *br.* © Abderit99/Fotolia, *tl.* © Getty Images/Hemera Technologies/Thinkstock, *mtm.* © Aaron Amat/Fotolia, *mtr.* © Oleg Shelomentsev/Fotolia, *mbl.* © r-o-x-o-r/Fotolia, *mbm.* © Getty Images/Hemera Technologies/Thinkstock, *bl.* © Michael Kempf/Fotolia, *bm.* © Marcin Sadlowski/Fotolia, *mr.* © Elaine Barker/Fotolia. 33: *Acrs2.* © Hemera Technologies/Thinkstock, *Acrs7.* © Henk Bentlage/Fotolia, *Acrs7.* © Yxowert/Fotolia, *Dwn5.* © Lisa Turay/Fotolia, *Acrs4.* © Maksym Gorpenyuk/Thinkstock, *Acrs6.* © Leah-Anne Thompson/Fotolia, *Acrs4.* © Aaron Amat/Fotolia, *Dwn6.* © Getty Images/Hemera Technologies/Thinkstock, *Dwn1.* © Elaine Barker/Fotolia. 37: © John R. Amelia/Fotolia. 39: *bml.* © Brand X Pictures/Thinkstock, *br.* © Jupiterimages/Thinkstock, *tl.* © Stockbyte/Thinkstock, *tml.* © Olga Sapegina/Fotolia, *tmr.* © Mario Beauregard/Fotolia, *tr.* © Imate/Fotolia, *ml.* © Getty Images/Jupiterimages/Thinkstock, *mml.* © Sotern/Fotolia, *mmr.* © Graça Victoria/Fotolia, *mr.* © Picture Partners/Fotolia, *bl.* © Sharpshot/Fotolia, *bmr.* © Borys Shevchuk/Fotolia. 40: *tl.* © Jupiterimages/Thinkstock, *tm.* © Little Tomato Studio/Fotolia, *tm.* © Picture Partners/Fotolia, *tr.* © Sotern/Fotolia, *mtl.* © Stockbyte/Thinkstock, *mtm.* © Close Encounters/Fotolia, *mtr.* © Borys Shevchuk/Fotolia, *mbl.* © Imate/Fotolia, *mbm.* © WINIKI/Fotolia, *mbr.* © Graça Victoria/Fotolia, *bl.* © Olga Sapegina/Fotolia, *bm.* © Getty Images/Jupiterimages/Thinkstock. 43: *tl.* © Eray/Fotolia, *bl.* © Hemera Technologies/Thinkstock, *bml.* © Gravicapa/Fotolia, *br.* © Lilyana Vynogradova/Fotolia, *tml.* © Ljupco Smokovski/Fotolia, *tmr.* © Jupiterimages/Thinkstock, *tr.* © Sneekerp/Fotolia, *mml.* © Svyatoslav Lypynskyy/Fotolia, *mml.* © Thinkstock, *mmr.* © PhotoObjects.net/Thinkstock, *mr.* © Elnur/Fotolia, *bmr.* © Iznogood/Fotolia. 46: *r.* © Eray/Fotolia, *l.* © Sergik/Fotolia, *mr.* © Picture Partners/Fotolia, *ml.* © Iznogood/Fotolia, *m.* © Elaine Barker/Fotolia. 53: *tl.* © Jupiterimages/Thinkstock, *mtl.* © DC Productions/Thinkstock, *mtmr.* © Yxowert/Fotolia, *mbml.* © Victoria Liu/Fotolia, *mbmr.* © Hemera Technologies/Thinkstock, *bml.* © Lilyana Vynogradova/Fotolia, *tml.* © r-o-x-o-r/Fotolia, *tmr.* © Comstock/Thinkstock, *tr.* © Ivan Stanic/Fotolia, *mtml.* © Thinkstock, *mtr.* © Hemera Technologies/Thinkstock, *mbl.* © Comstock/Thinkstock, *mbr.* © Getty Images/Hemera Technologies/Thinkstock, *bl.* © Sharpshot/Fotolia, *bmr.* © Oneuser/Fotolia, *br.* © Michael Gray/Fotolia. 56: *m.* © Liquidlibrary/Thinkstock. 58: *l.*

© Azurelaroux/Fotolia, *ml.* © Ia_64/Fotolia, *r.* © Kelpfish/Fotolia, *mr.* © ioannis kounadeas/Fotolia. 59: *ml.* © DC Productions/Thinkstock, *l.* © Aleksandr Ugorenkov/Fotolia, *mr.* © Anetta/Fotolia, *r.* © Comstock/Thinkstock. 60: *l.* © Getty Images/Jupiterimages/Thinkstock, *mr.* © M. Camerin/Fotolia, *r.* © James Steidl/Fotolia, *ml.* © Iznogood/Fotolia. 70: *tm.* © Kushnirov Avraham/Fotolia, *tr.* © Petr Masek/Fotolia, *tl.* © Alexandra Karamyshev/Fotolia, *bm.* © Stockbyte/Thinkstock, *br.* © Getty Images/Hemera Technologies/Thinkstock, *bl.* © moonrun/Fotolia. 71: *bl.* © Kushnirov Avraham/Fotolia, *br.* © Pixland/Thinkstock, *tl.* © Stockbyte/Thinkstock, *tm.* © Close Encounters/Fotolia, *tr.* © James Steidl/Fotolia, *bm.* © Milosluz/Fotolia. 73: *tl.* © Tschmittjohn/Fotolia, *bl.* © PhotoZA/Fotolia, *tm.* © Lev Olkha/Fotolia, *tr.* © vlorzor/Fotolia, *bm.* © Ionescu Bogdan/Fotolia, *br.* © imrek/Fotolia. 75: *bml.* © Victoria Liu/Fotolia, *tl.* © Borys Shevchuk/Fotolia, *tml.* © Getty Images/Hemera Technologies/Thinkstock, *tmr.* © Brand X Pictures/Thinkstock, *tr.* © Anetta/Fotolia, *ml.* © Solodovnikova Elena/Fotolia, *mml.* © Thinkstock, *mmr.* © 0neuser/Fotolia. © Milosluz/Fotolia, *bl.* © Alexandra Karamyshev/Fotolia, *bmr.* © Brand X Pictures/Thinkstock, *br.* © James Steidl/Fotolia. 81: *t.* © Chee-Onn Leong/Fotolia, *b.* © Roy Grogan/Fotolia. 82: *t.* © Jupiterimages/Thinkstock, *b.* © Galyna Andrushko/Fotolia. 83: *tmr.* © Victoria Liu/Fotolia, *mtml.* © Abderit99/Fotolia, *bl.* © Petr Masek/Fotolia, *tl.* © Sergik/Fotolia, *tml.* © Anetta/Fotolia, *tr.* © Getty Images/Hemera Technologies/Thinkstock, *mtl.* © Lev Olkha/Fotolia, *mtmr.* © Alexandra Karamyshev/Fotolia, *mbl.* © Borys Shevchuk/Fotolia, *mbml.* © Milosluz/Fotolia, *mbr.* © Rtimages/Fotolia, *mbmr.* © Thinkstock, *bml.* © Sotern/Fotolia, *bmr.* © Sneekerp/Fotolia, *br.* © James Steidl/Fotolia, *mtr.* © Iznogood/Fotolia. 85: © Mike & Valerie Mille/Fotolia. 89: *tmr.* © Shariff Che'Lah/Fotolia, *mmr.* © Duncan Noakes/Fotolia, *bml.* © George Doyle/Thinkstock, *ml.* © Lilyana Vynogradova/Fotolia, *tl.* © Felinda/Fotolia, *tml.* © fotogal/Fotolia, *tr.* © Cphoto/Fotolia, *mml.* © Svyatoslav Lypynskyy/Fotolia, *mr.* © Hemera Technologies/Thinkstock, *bl.* © Brand X Pictures/Thinkstock, *bmr.* © cretolamna/Fotolia, *br.* © Irochka/Fotolia. 91: *t.* © Jupiterimages/Thinkstock, *bm.* © Paul Hakimata/Fotolia, *ml.* © Bruce MacQueen/Fotolia, *tm.* © Hemera Technologies/Getty Images/Thinkstock, *tr.* © Zedcor Wholly Owned/ Getty Images/Thinkstock, *m.* © Feng Yu/Fotolia, *mr.* © Elnur/Fotolia, *bl.* © Paul Moore/Fotolia, *br.* © Iosif Szasz-Fabian/Fotolia. 93: *bl.* © Yodanet Company/Fotolia, *tl.* © Jose Manuel Gelpi/Fotolia, *tm.* © Blaz Kure/Fotolia, *tr.* © blue eye/Fotolia, *ml.* © Getty Images/Hemera Technologies/ Thinkstock, *m.* © Cphoto/Fotolia, *mr.* © Brand X Pictures/Thinkstock, *bm.* © Jupiterimages/Thinkstock, *br.* © Leonid Nyshko/Fotolia. 95: *tm.* © Cora Reed/Fotolia, *tr.* © Petr Masek/Fotolia, *br.* © Christian Musat/Fotolia, *tl.* © Johnny Lye/Fotolia, *ml.* © Ablestock.com/Thinkstock, *m.* © Andres Rodriguez/Fotolia, *mr.* © r-o-x-o-r/Fotolia, *bm.* © nedjenn/Fotolia, *bml.* © Andrew S./Fotolia. 99: *t.* © Getty Images/Comstock Images/ Thinkstock, *b.* © JENNY SOLOMON/Fotolia. 101: *mr.* © Cheryl Davis/Fotolia, *r.* © Jupiterimages/Thinkstock, *l.* © Volff/Fotolia, *ml.* © Riverwalker/ Fotolia. 102: *tmr.* © Cheryl Davis/Fotolia, *bml.* © Jupiterimages/Thinkstock, *tl.* © Volff/Fotolia, *tml.* © Tatty/Fotolia, *tr.* © Michael Flippo/Fotolia, *bl.* © George Dolgikh/Fotolia, *bmr.* © Hemera Technologies/Getty Images/Thinkstock, *br.* © Michael Shake/Fotolia. 103: *br.* © Digital Vision/ Thinkstock, *tl.* © Homydesign/Fotolia, *tm.* © Auremar/Fotolia, *tr.* © Berean/Fotolia, *bl.* © Marietjie Opperman/Fotolia, *bm.* © Photodisc/Thinkstock. 104: *tl.* © blue eye/Fotolia, *tr.* © Ivan Stanic/Fotolia, *bl.* © Getty Images/Hemera Technologies/Thinkstock, *br.* © Feng Yu/Fotolia. 105: *tr.* © Jim Mills/Fotolia, *mml.* © Stephen Finn/Fotolia, *mr.* © Hemera Technologies/Thinkstock, *bml.* © Stockbyte/Thinkstock, *br.* © MTC Media/Fotolia, *mmr.* © Yahia Loukkal/Fotolia, *tl.* © Hemera Technologies/Thinkstock, *ml.* © Hemera Technologies/Getty Images/Thinkstock, *tm.* © Yahia Loukkal/ Fotolia, *ml.* © Getty Images/Comstock Images/Thinkstock, *bl.* © Efired/Fotolia, *bmr.* © Ellypoo/Thinkstock. 106: *tl.* © Comstock/Thinkstock, *tr.* © Stephen Finn/Fotolia, *bl.* © Shariff Che'Lah/Fotolia, *bm.* © Hemera Technologies/Thinkstock, *tm.* © Lamax/Fotolia, *br.* © Getty Images/Comstock Images/Thinkstock. 108: *tr.* © Tom Brakefield/Thinkstock, *mbl.* © Duncan Noakes/Fotolia, *mtr.* © Lilyana Vynogradova/Fotolia, *tl.* © Homydesign/ Fotolia, *tm.* © Comstock/Thinkstock, *mtl.* © PhotoObjects.net/Thinkstock, *mtm.* © Hemera Technologies/Getty Images/Thinkstock, *mbm.* © Stockbyte/Thinkstock, *mbr.* © Jiri Hera/Fotolia, *tl.* © Elnur/Fotolia, *bm.* © PhotoGrapHie/Fotolia, *br.* © Ana Vasileva/Fotolia. 114: *mtm.* © Jupiterimages/Thinkstock, *tl.* © Paul Murphy/Fotolia, *tm.* © Otmar Smit/Fotolia, *ml.* © Le Do/Fotolia, *mtl.* © Eric Isselée/Fotolia, *mbl.* © O.M/ Fotolia, *mtr.* © Ulga/Fotolia, *mbm.* © MAXFX/Fotolia, *mbr.* © Ivaylo Ivanov/Fotolia, *bl.* © Maxim Loskutnikov/Fotolia, *br.* © Leonid Nyshko/Fotolia, *bm.* © Sebastian Kaulitzki/Fotolia. 115: *tr.* © Jupiterimages/Thinkstock, *bml.* © Cora Reed/Fotolia, *tr.* © O.M/Fotolia, *tl.* © Zedcor Wholly Owned/ Getty Images/Thinkstock, *ml.* © Elnur/Fotolia, *tmr.* © Jupiterimages/Thinkstock, *br.* © StarJumper/Fotolia, *mml.* © Robynmac/Fotolia, *mmr.* © Nymph/Fotolia, *mr.* © Comstock/Thinkstock, *bl.* © Hemera Technologies/Getty Images/Thinkstock, *bmr.* © Riverwalker/Fotolia. 121: *mtl.* © Xavier Marchant/Fotolia, *mtr.* © Abderit99/Fotolia, *mbmr.* © Philippe Leridon/Fotolia, *mbr.* © Archmen/Fotolia, *tl.* © Hemera Technologies/Getty Images/Thinkstock, *tmr.* © blue eye/Fotolia, *tr.* © Ivaylo Ivanov/Fotolia, *mtml.* © Marc Dietrich/Fotolia, *mtmr.* © Henryk Olszewski/Fotolia, *mbl.* © Ilandrea/Fotolia, *mbml.* © Tatty/Fotolia, *bl.* © Getty Images/PhotoObjects.net/Thinkstock, *bml.* © Vladimir Chernyanski/Fotolia, *bmr.* © Jac/ Fotolia, *br.* © Ugocutilli/Fotolia, *tml.* © imaginando/Fotolia. 123: © Irochka/Fotolia, *tr.* © Michael Shake/Fotolia, *ml.* © Barbara Penoyar/ Thinkstock, *mr.* © Lane Erickson/Fotolia, *bl.* © Stockbyte/Thinkstock, *br.* © Philippe Devanne/Fotolia. 127: © shalltron/Fotolia. 128: © Corepics/ Fotolia. 129: © reb/Fotolia. 135: *mr.* © Ablestock.com/Thinkstock, *tl.* © Roger Scott/Fotolia, *mmr.* © Austinadams/Fotolia, *tm.* © Bruce MacQueen/ Fotolia, *ml.* © HP_Photo/Fotolia, *mml.* © PhotoObjects.net/Thinkstock, *bml.* © Tommy/Fotolia, *bl.* © Alx/Thinkstock, *bmr.* © Hemera Technologies/ Getty Images/Thinkstock, *bmr.* © Les Cunliffe/Fotolia, *br.* © Ronen/Fotolia. 136: *tm.* © Ablestock.com/Thinkstock, *tr.* © Roger Scott/Fotolia, *tr.* © Bruce MacQueen/Fotolia, *bl.* © Les Cunliffe/Fotolia, *bm.* © Hemera Technologies/Getty Images/Thinkstock, *br.* © PhotoObjects.net/Thinkstock. 139: *t.* © Tom Brakefield/Thinkstock, *b.* © Jens Klingebiel/Fotolia. 140: *t.* © Jupiterimages/Thinkstock, *b.* © Jupiterimages/Thinkstock. 141: *mtm.* © Roger Scott/Fotolia, *mbl.* © Paul Murphy/Fotolia, *tl.* © Yodanet Company/Fotolia, *tr.* © Jupiterimages/Thinkstock, *m.* © Hemera Technologies/ Thinkstock, *mr.* © Tom Brakefield/Thinkstock, *mbm.* © Agphotographer/Fotolia, *mbr.* © Archmen/Fotolia, *tm.* © Andres Rodriguez/Fotolia, *mtl.* © Vinicius Tupinamba/Fotolia, *mtr.* © Ivaylo Ivanov/Fotolia, *ml.* © Marietjie Opperman/Fotolia, *bm.* © Paul Moore/Fotolia, *br.* © Stef Rauza/Fotolia, *bl.* © imaginando/Fotolia. 143: © NASA/courtesy of nasaimages.org. 144: © NASA. 151: © NASA/courtesy of nasaimages.org. 153: *tl.* © Steve Byland/Fotolia, *tr.* © Margo/Fotolia, *ml.* © Linn Currie/Fotolia, *mtl.* © Stockbyte/Thinkstock, *mbl.* © Aleksandr Ugorenkov/Fotolia, *mbl.* © Blaz Kure/ Fotolia, *br.* © fotogal/Fotolia, *bl.* © Atropat/Fotolia. 154: *tl.* © Jose Manuel Gelpi/Fotolia, *tr.* © Jose Manuel Gelpi/Fotolia, *bl.* © Getty Images/ Jupiterimages/Thinkstock, *br.* © Yuri Arcurs/Fotolia. 161: *t.* © Alexandr Ozerov/Fotolia, *b.* © NASA. 170: *tl.* © debr22pics/Fotolia, *tm.* © Ivaylo Ivanov/Fotolia, *tr.* © Konnov Leonid/Fotolia. 171: *bl.* © Paul Murphy/Fotolia, *br.* © Jupiterimages/Thinkstock, *bm.* © Konnov Leonid/Fotolia. 174: © NASA. 175: *t.* © NASA, *b.* © NASA. 176: *t.* © Kim Dismukes/NASA, *b.* © NASA. 177: *tm.* © Sonya Etchison/Fotolia, *mtl.* © Vgm/Fotolia, *bm.* © Margo/Fotolia, *mbr.* © David De Lossy/Thinkstock, *tl.* © Stockbyte/Thinkstock, *tr.* © Berean/Fotolia, *mtm.* © Maxim Loskutnikov/Fotolia, *mtr.* © Michellepix/Fotolia, *bl.* © Cantor p/Pannatto/Fotolia, *tm.* © Ints/Fotolia, *br.* © Jacek Chabraszewski/Fotolia, *mbl.* © Atropat/Fotolia. 180: *m.* © Michelle Robek/Fotolia. 181: *br.* © Linous/Fotolia, *tl.* © Kelpfish/Fotolia, *tr.* © cretolamna/Fotolia, *ml.* © Mikko Pitkänen/Fotolia, *m.* © Pezography/ Fotolia, *bl.* © Aidaricci/Fotolia, *bm.* © Hemera Technologies/Getty Images/Thinkstock, *mr.* © Close Encounters/Fotolia, *tm.* © ioannis kounadeas/ Fotolia. 183: *tl.* © Tschmittjohn/Fotolia, *tm.* © PhotoZA/Fotolia, *mbl.* © Enrico Scarsi/Fotolia, *mbm.* © Monkey Business/Fotolia, *tr.* © imrek/Fotolia, *mtl.* © Solodovnikova Elena/Fotolia, *mtm.* © vlorzor/Fotolia, *mtr.* © Lev Olkha/Fotolia, *mbr.* © Ionescu Bogdan/Fotolia, *bl.* © Elnur/Fotolia, *bm.* © Feng Yu/Fotolia, *br.* © Hemera Technologies/Thinkstock. 184: © Jupiterimages/Thinkstock. 185: *2.* © Wild Geese/Fotolia, *1.* © Leslie Banks /123RF, *3.* © Lev Olkha/Fotolia, *4.* © Close Encounters/Fotolia, *5.* © Getty Images/Jupiterimages/Thinkstock, *6.* © Brand X Pictures/Thinkstock. 186: *tm.* © Alexford/Fotolia, *bl.* © Petr Masek/Fotolia, *br.* © Wild Geese/Fotolia, *tl.* © Alexandra Karamyshev/Fotolia, *tr.* © Lev Olkha/Fotolia, *b.* © Stockbyte/Thinkstock. 189: *t.* © Paco Ayala/Fotolia, *b.* © Hunta/Fotolia. 190: *t.* © Bastos/Fotolia, *b.* © Michael Gray/Fotolia. 192: *bl.* © Kasoga/ Fotolia, *bml.* © By-Studio/Fotolia, *bmr.* © dimch/Fotolia, *b.* © Marek/Fotolia. 194: *tl.* © Yang Yu/Fotolia, *tm.* © Berna Safoglu/Fotolia, *tr.* © Gene Lee/Fotolia, *bl.* © Ivan Gulei/Fotolia, *bm.* © Feng Yu/Fotolia, *br.* © NatUlrich/Fotolia. 197: *tr.* © Getty Images/Hemera Technologies/Thinkstock, *bl.* © Rozalin/Fotolia, *tl.* © Kasoga/Fotolia, *br.* © Berna Safoglu/Fotolia. 198: *tr.* © Dieter Spannknebel/Thinkstock, *mbr.* © Rozalin/Fotolia, *tm.* © Michel Bazin/Fotolia, *tl.* © Marie-Thérèse GUIHAL/Fotolia, *tm.* © Feng Yu/Fotolia, *mtl.* © Yang Yu/Fotolia, *mtl.* © Hemera Technologies/Thinkstock, *mtm.* © Berna Safoglu/Fotolia, *mbl.* © By-Studio/Fotolia, *mbm.* © jovica antoski/Fotolia, *bl.* © Du an Zidar/Fotolia, *br.* © NatUlrich/Fotolia. 199: © DX/Fotolia. 203: *tm.* © Digital Vision/Thinkstock, *tr.* © Route66Photography/Fotolia, *br.* © David De Lossy/Thinkstock, *tl.* © Simone van den Berg/Fotolia, *mtr.* © Emilia Stasiak/Fotolia, *bm.* © Stockbyte/Thinkstock, *mbl.* © Comstock/Thinkstock, *mbl.* © Eyewave/Fotolia, *br.* © Tein/Fotolia, *bl.* © Giuseppe_R/Fotolia. 207: *t.* © Roman Sigaev/Fotolia, *tm.* © Leslie Banks /123RF, *tr.* © Jiri Hera/Fotolia, *ml.* © John Holst/Fotolia, *m.* © Grigoriy Lukyanov/Fotolia, *mr.* © a4stockphotos/Fotolia, *bl.* © ZTS/Fotolia, *bm.* © Arpad Nagy-Bagoly/Fotolia, *br.* © Coprid/Fotolia. 209: © Jupiterimages/Thinkstock. 213: *tl.* © Alexford/Fotolia, *tm.* © Digital Vision/Thinkstock, *mr.* © Rozalin/Fotolia, *tr.* © Jiri Hera/Fotolia, *ml.* © Elnur/ Fotolia, *m.* © Ia_64/Fotolia, *bl.* © Zee/Fotolia, *bm.* © Feng Yu/Fotolia, *br.* © Getty Images/Jupiterimages/Thinkstock. 219: *background.* © Przemys-law Moranski/Fotolia. 224: *mtm.* © Jupiterimages/Thinkstock, *mbm.* © Hallgerd/Fotolia, *tl.* © Jacek Chabraszewski/Fotolia, *tr.* © JJ'Studio/Fotolia, *tr.* © Tatagatta/Fotolia, *mtl.* © Andrey Zametalov/Fotolia, *mtr.* © BananaStock/Thinkstock, *mbl.* © Alexandre Zveiger/Fotolia, *mbr.* © Stef Rauza/ Fotolia, *bl.* © Noam/Fotolia, *bm.* © Superstock, *br.* © Alexey Stiop/Fotolia. 232: *tm.* © Comstock Images/Thinkstock, *mbl.* © Comstock/Thinkstock, *mbm.* © Jupiterimages/Thinkstock, *mbr.* © Gary/Fotolia, *bl.* © Agphotographer/Fotolia, *bm.* © Jim Mills/Fotolia, *br.* © Kraig Scarbinsky/Thinkstock, *tr.* © Viktor/Fotolia, *mtl.* © Getty Images/Jupiterimages/Thinkstock, *mtm.* © Jupiterimages/Thinkstock, *br.* © Getty Images/PhotoObjects.net/ Thinkstock, *bm.* © Giuseppe_R/Fotolia. 237: *t.* © Petrosya/Fotolia, *b.* © Aristidis Tsinaroglou/www.smartmagna.com/Superstock. 238: *t.* © Petro-syan/Fotolia, *b.* © Hervé Rouveure/Fotolia. 240: *tr.* © Tony Campbell/Fotolia, *tl.* © Kushnirov Avraham/Fotolia, *tm.* © Close Encounters/Fotolia, *tm.* © Valua Vitaly/Fotolia, *br.* © Michael Greenberg/Thinkstock, *bm.* © Elaine Barker/Fotolia.